THE
STARFIELD PRESS
WORLDSTORY
2013
TREASURY

Oklahoma City, OK

WORLDSTORY 2013

Copyright © 2014 Starfield Press
www.StarfieldPress.com

Paperback ISBN: 978-0615964478

All rights reserved. No part of this publication may be reproduced, distributed, or transmitted in any form or by any means, including photocopying, recording, or other electronic or mechanical methods, without prior written permission of the publisher, except in the case of brief quotations embodied in critical reviews and certain other noncommercial uses permitted by copyright law.

Each story contained within these pages remains the copyright of the participant who submitted it for this project. They may still use their work however and whenever they wish.

Cover design by Lloyd Matthew Thompson

WORLDSTORY 2013

• CONTENTS •

INTRODUCTION 11

THE BIRTHING 21
— ELENA FLORES

CHALLENGE 25
— CHALLENGED

THE BALANCE 27
— MELISSA RAE THOMPSON

THE YEAR I LOST MYSELF 31
— AGATHE BJØRNSDATTER MOLVIK

THE MESSAGE 35
— SARAH KRAJEWSKI WEBB

A LEAP OF FAITH 43
— SHANNON LAACKMANN

EXPECTATIONS AND FEARS 49
— NIKKI BEARD

SPREADING CALM 55
— GARY MOLLOY

PERCEPTIONS 59
— SHELLY WILSON

DECISIONS 71
  — NATALIE WHEELER

REACHING FARTHER 81
  — LISA BACHRACH-ZEANKOWSKI

FIRSTHAND DARKNESS 91
  — LLOYD MATTHEW THOMPSON

THE VENUS-PLUTO CYCLE 97
  — BRIG

THE WEEK 111
  — MONICA ROLLER

BENEVOLENT MESSAGE 137
  — EDWARD FELICIANO

THE PRESENCE OF SPIRIT 157
  — LORI HOMSTAD

• INTRODUCTION •

You ARE NOW HOLDING in your hands the first in a long line of treasuries from *Starfield Press* (I have seen the future!) that will each play a role in the transformation of this world.

The biggest key to this claim?

Each one will be written by *you*: the regular person, the brother, the sister, the mirrored reflection of all around you.

You see, in a world where true separation is impossible to find, everything that happens, everything that is decided, and everything that one does affects another person, place, or thing — or *all* of the above.

Yet this does not apply only to the so-called "negative" aspects; the just-as-equal "positive" actions yank on the web of life, and affect all else in existence just as much. When one opens and allows a vulnerability and a healing to occur, the way is opened for others to open and heal as well. When one shatters their way through an emotional, mental, or spiritual wall, the interconnected wall is that much weaker for the next being to smash through and find the next step in their own enlightenment.

And so the concept of WORLDSTORY was born.

A major goal of *Starfield Press* is to inspire growth and expansion via stories, whether the story is a non-fiction, a fiction, or a creative river of words flowing from the depths of one's soul, as poetry is. Its tagline, *Everyone's World Has a Story to Tell*, captures these intentions beautifully, for a thousand people could witness the exact same event, and each one's story recounting that event would be absolutely different, colored and flavored by their own experiences and energies — and it takes **all** facets of a diamond to *make* the diamond, no?

The goal of the WORLDSTORY project is to relate to each other in unity; to encourage and inspire through the sharing of personal stories, trials, lessons, blessings, and growth; and to offer a space of healing for both those doing the writing (and therefore processing and purging), and for those reading.

And the right people will read the right words at exactly the right time they need it. That's how this world works.

Capturing our experiences in writing also serves as excellent documentation of our progress and process—who knows where we will be even next year, much less in ten years? When we are able to go back and read where we were at *this* time, what an experience of clarity we will have; we will be able to see more exactly *how* we got there!

In this way it is not a *his*tory or a *her*story, but a *world*story.

Another excellent reason to convert our reflections into writing is the value of translating it itself. Just as our eyes send inherently empty and meaningless visual impulses to our brain, and then it is our brain that inspects and assigns a label or meaning to the image and translates it into something we can understand, the same goes for the reverse. What is held inside us is composed of layers and layers of everything from thought forms to emotional and felt forms. How can that be communicated to others? All those layers cannot easily be embedded on the paper so others feel it for themselves—it must be translated into symbols that *can* be understood by others: words! The very act of analyzing and breaking down what is inside us in order to convert it into something others can understand makes us look at it from even more angles that we may not have before.

2013 was the first full year after the much-anticipated 2012 Shift — what better time to begin a project such as *WORLDSTORY?*

There is no denying that things *have* changed in this world, and shifted on every level. Whether the "2012 Shift" was an actual event, or if it was merely the intentions and expectations wrapped around it by millions of beings that manifested the shift, there *was* a shift.

Accountability and responsibility seem to be the major theme everyone is dealing with at this time. What was hidden is now being exposed, what is done is now being called to be owned, and what is desired is now being manifested at blurring speeds — which many are quickly learning to make sure they specify exact details of what it is they want.

Many, many people are having an extremely difficult time with these new energies. All over this world, people are experiencing heightened emotions, mental and physical breakdowns, and what feels like crisis after crisis. Some are even giving up altogether, choosing to leave the planet at this time!

I've seen people who have been steady-tempered for years and years suddenly flip and lose their minds, going crazy and becoming absolutely unpredictable.

I've seen others meet this wall (this tsunami?) with determination and resolve, and manage to pierce through its challenges, emerging on the other side shining and purified.

And I've seen others still simply sail through the turning tides without a scratch or problem whatsoever!

Everyone's experience is relative to and depends on the rest of their factors, choices, and previous experiences — their programming, if you will.

So what did *your* 2013 hold for you?

It's never too late to meditate upon, and record your own experiences, whether it is done as a part of this project or not — and we highly encourage you to do so!

Perhaps some or all of the stories in this edition will speak to you, show you that you are not the only one in a certain situation, or uplift you to the heights that *you* need to reach your next level.

The arrangement of these stories has been chosen at random by my three year old daughter, allowing the Universe to select the order in which they should appear from the mouth of a babe—or from the drawing of paper slips in her Daddy's hat.

I encourage you to absorb these stories with an open Heart, open Eyes, and an open Mind.

Many blessings!

Lloyd Matthew Thompson
Editor, *Starfield Press*
January 2014

WORLDSTORY 2013

• THE BIRTHING •

WE ALL EXPECTED SOMETHING dramatic to happen on December 21, 2012… some of us were disappointed, some of us were relieved the world didn't end, and for others—like me—the shift started occurring gently, painfully slow, and inevitably.

Looking to the year behind, and even further back into my life, I find myself asking the question, "Who *was* that person in my head who had a hold of me for nearly three decades?"

December 21, 2012, was the moment of conception, the moment I conceived the understanding that there *is* a seed of something deeper, clearer, and enormous in me. A dear friend and loving guide called this feeling *being pregnant with myself.*

In the First trimester, from Winter Solstice 2012 until the Spring Equinox, there was little change, just a budding feeling that something was different, and a silent acknowledgment that my life would never be the same. New explorations and deeper practices opened my eyes to the extraordinarily tight grip my mind had on my perception. I saw it clearly, like a giant blob of sticky silly putty draping itself over me and changing my perception into a vortex of endless assumptions and judgments.

"What I think others think is still what I think" was the shock of a thought that brought me back into this world and put me on guard as to what is true and what is just a trick of the mind. I saw myself, my soul, lying down on the bottom of a deep, dark dungeon, weak, abandoned, and barely alive, chained by my own ignorance.

I was barely breathing, but willing to fight for my liberation from the oppression of illusion.

Slowly and painfully, the journey continued through Spring, awakening to my new understanding, practicing awareness and failing miserably many times, slipping back into the fog of old habits, old judgments, old conception.

Many times I wept and wished to slip back into my ignorance, not knowing that there was a way out—and also knowing ignorance was no longer possible.

They say awareness is enough... it is far from enough, and yet once we are aware, going back is no longer an option.

On and on this process went, taking one step forward and then two steps back... melting resistance just to find it in another place... finding an answer just so ten thousand more questions can pop up... connecting and practicing, drawing strength only from the place of pure Love that I knew existed in me... sometimes only blindly trusting in it.

The Summer Solstice brought new challenges, more help, and I saw my spirit family slowly gathering around me, all of us holding hands and walking each other home.

I had to open my eyes to see that I am not the only one on this path, that I had never been the only one, but the fog of the mind, the illusion of separation had convinced me that way.

We gathered in circles, we prayed, we danced, we cried, and we sang walking together and helping each other. And that in itself was one of the greatest transformations, the greatest shift in my consciousness — in our global consciousness.

We were ready to soar, spread our wings, and change the world. We could feel the quickening, the great shift the Fall Equinox was bringing: the birth of our new selves. We danced under the moon, and sang the new songs breathed into us.

And there it was: my soul slipped out of the

darkness and into this world, and I was ready to fly... Only to realize I need to learn to move my fingers and my toes first, to learn to crawl, to command my voice, and to get my body to obey me.

And now, on the verge of the Winter Solstice once again, I feel a little more confident, a little more in command of my new expanded and birthed self. I feel ready to plunge into the darkness of the winter, this time fully aware; diving into the coldest and most dusty corners of myself, nurturing and nourishing that which has already grown, so I can emerge once again with the spring sun and keep on walking home, holding the hand of the whole universe.

Elena Flores
New York, USA
EnlightenmentSmellsLikeChocolate.blogspot.com

• CHALLENGE •

THIS ONE WORD HAS always described my life. 2013 showed itself to be no different.

The most rewarding challenge this year has been in my workplace. In the midst of a downsized department I learned that if I can find new ways to accomplish the tasks given me, I can rise to the challenge and be a success! Successful challenge always begins from being able to think outside the box.

The most despairing challenge came when my eighteen-year-old son declared himself an "adult" and left home against my pleading—with no plan of action or financial stability, not to mention one more year of high school to complete. This challenge has yet to see an end, but I am positive that the challenge to be consistent with boundaries and showing tough love will see this challenge through to the end. I've never had to think outside the box *this* way with any other child, and I admit it hurts; but I am confident this is where the challenge lies, and will see it through.

Challenges are good for us, whether we think so or not.

Embrace the moments of challenge set in your path each day of life.

Grow, learn, and change for the best you can be!

Challenged
Oklahoma, USA

• THE BALANCE •

2013 WAS A HELLUVA year!

Life, simply put, is not simple.

There is no consistency that a mere mortal can see. Overlapping details create an ever-unfolding order that often appears as chaos.

When 2013 started, I believed that I was in control of my life. Control is an illusion. We cannot control what other people think or do. Focusing on my own actions and thoughts is a full time job.

Nostalgia hit me hard this year. I begged for mercy. For a while, I pleaded, *"Why me? Why us?"*

I was left sobbing in the trenches.

The truth is, the Universe is *not* my enemy.

I can be my own very worst enemy, especially when I allow others to have power over me by emotionally reacting.

Mindfully responding takes more breath and thought, but it is a far better place to reach out towards a problem.

I learned (and am still learning) that life is not out to get me. Life is not a scary figure, squatting behind a bush, and wearing a dark trench coat. By allowing myself to erase this illusion from my mind, I am able to focus on what is known.

I may still not understand it, but that is okay.

To have any real answers, we need to see everything in its entirety. Only a pin-point of explanation is ever truly given to us. That seems very little to base a solid opinion upon.

There is an outdated idea that good things happen to good people.

Wrong.

What a repetitious lie.

Some of the best people experience the greatest hardships. Some of the worst people have the best luck: Jesus Christ was crucified, Mahatma Gandhi was beaten and imprisoned, and Nelson Mandela spent over 27 years in prison.

Karma is not about punishment, but cause and effect.

There are natural consequences for the things we do. The universe demands a balanced scale.

STARFIELD PRESS

We may not be balancing our scale, but instead helping to balance the universal scale.

Melissa Rae Thompson
Oklahoma, USA
FoxandOwl.net

• THE YEAR I LOST MYSELF •

2013 MUST HAVE BEEN the hardest of my thirty-one years alive. Not because anything particularly dramatic happened, nothing more than the usual stuff anyway. No, 2013 wasn't particularly bad; it was just particularly *difficult.*

2012 had been a year of immense hope and anticipation for the new time to come. I, of course, knew that I wouldn't wake up to peace on Earth and people dancing in the streets, but still there was that teeny-tiny chance that it actually would happen that way. At least that something major and life-changing would occur, something that would mark the new era big time, something that would make me feel reassured for being on the right track, and perhaps something that would sweep some of those annoying rocks off my path. It didn't happen like that.

Rather, 2013 was the year I lost myself.

Yes, the old sense of me seemed to vanish somewhere along the way. I cannot pinpoint it to a special time or event—I just know it happened.

I had died.

And as with any loss, you grieve.

I mean, I used to be a fun-loving, playful girl who enjoyed to sip her Scotch and who took pride in her independence. I also took pride in my large record collection, my pretty things and my sense of uniqueness. I had built a character around myself that I had perfected to the tee. It was a character that people fell for, that I used to love to show off and that had pretty much become what I wanted it to be.

Suddenly, it meant nothing to me anymore. I felt bored with myself. I felt like I was running on fixed tracks, on old habits, like I had built my life around projections that bore no meaning any longer. Presenting myself in the old way made me feel like a liar, like a fake. I was nothing. I was a great big pile of nothingness, a blur. I had no idea where I was heading, or even where I was.

So, I had the sorrow of the loss of the old me, who I, after all, *had* been pretty fond of, and then I had the confusion of not knowing who the fuck I was anymore! Oh yes—it was also the year I started swearing.

When something dies, something new is born; it is just the natural way things work. But birthing can be painful, and the worst is it can take a great deal of time. I know this because when I gave birth to my son, the hardest part wasn't the pain itself, it was that it dragged out for so long. I never knew how long it would be, what to expect next, and nothing really seemed to move. It was the not knowing that was the worst, the feeling of standing still, of having no control, of impatience.

And this was 2013 for me: Being in labor and not quite getting there.

At least that is what it felt like, and that is why 2013 felt so difficult.

Yet this still isn't the full story. I *did* lose something: I lost a sense of self, and a sense of direction. I had become nothing, at least nothing I could define in terms of possessions or preferences. I had died, and not quite fully been born anew.

However, it wasn't my becoming that was missing, it was my acceptance.

Truth is that I already am. There is nothing I need to do or change, there is nothing to aim for, nowhere to go. That is the greatest gift of all, yet it is the hardest gift to accept.

It means that I am… fine.

It means that I don't need to buy things or achieve things to be me. I already am.

I am still working on it—the being fine part—it does take some getting used to.

Every morning when I wake up, I remind myself *things are okay*, otherwise it's so easy to fall back into the old habit of running somewhere else.

Being me is a choice I have to make moment to moment, but at least I've become aware of it as an option, because I hadn't really been before.

2013 was the year I found myself.

Agathe Bjørnsdatter Molvik
Nordland, Norway
TheUtopian.net

• THE MESSAGE •

I WOKE THIS MORNING with one message. It is the message that I get constantly, but today it seemed to have more energy behind it, a new drive. It is the message I got when I went to a crystal healer for the first time and didn't really know why I was going. I had just followed the signs.

The message was to share my journey.

Simple, straightforward—just be me and share it with others.

The specifics of this message were to write about my awakening, to put the information out there. It is energy combining with other energies.

Now, I am not an expert; I am very comfortable identifying as a beginner, and I have found great freedom in that. I have seen there are many things I want to experience in this incarnation—goals, wishes, and desires that I want to fulfill. But I believe there is value in everything and every place, position, and location that we find ourselves, whether it is on this physical plane, or a place we have visited via non-physical means.

I am truly enamored with the myriad ways that we find ourselves, that we create situations, that we attract people and that we react to our creations. And if you find yourself in a place that is undesirable to you, I hear you. I have been there. I have created it multiple times, and I love you.

And I have released the desire to understand everything as I am experiencing it. I support your release as well, if you possess such a desire.

As I write this, there is a spirit with me I can only identify as a pink flame. I do not know what that means, but I point it out because I desire to share with you an experience that my mind cannot understand using reason. I desire to share with you that going through this human experience, creating in a linear manner fashioned by time *is* possible, and we do not have to understand it as it happens.

Of course, my ego screams, *"Go to Google! Look up pink flames! Who has channeled this? What does it mean?"* But it has been made clear to me that I wish to experience this in my own way, learning to follow my own intuition.

The message I am guided to share is how I came to my awakening.

The story is that I spent most of my teenage and adult life miserable. I had several traumatic, out of the norm life experiences. I suffered from mental illness, multiple addictions, and forms of abuse, depression, and lack of support as I perceived it. I tried many traditional and non-traditional, methods to get help. I learned to take what I could use from each, and as wise people say, "Leave the rest." So I did.

Many times I told myself that if things didn't work out I could always kill myself. But I postponed it many times in the hope that I would find something new. I practiced those things that worked for me until the situation I found myself was so undesirable that I became willing— Willing to change, willing to listen to anyone, willing to listen to my body, willing to try new things even if I had no idea how they would work out. I set aside everything my ego said about how right I was, how everything in my life was screaming that this was how life worked, how I knew how the world really operated.

I was willing to set aside being right for the desire to have peace.

It didn't come overnight. It didn't even come in two weeks or two months. But once I was willing, I had to be honest with myself and with other people. I stopped trying to manipulate people to get what I wanted. I wasn't interested in little white lies or great big giant ones. I wanted to be authentic; I wanted to know *me.*

What I found was a change in myself at first. If someone asked me how I was, it was a difficult question in the beginning. I felt awful and I didn't want to tell other people how I felt. I avoided the topic. Eventually, I was able to be honest, but brief: "I'm not 100% today but the day's not over yet." I was not a positive thinker, but I had one in my life who was having amazing results, and I was throwing everything I had into it. I am very grateful for her today.

I started being completely honest with people. If they asked me if I wanted to do something that I really didn't want to do, I told them in the kindest way I could think of without making excuses: "I would love to spend time with you. Can we go to the movies instead?" Then I left the decision with them. And when things didn't go the way I would have liked them to go, I took care of myself, because that didn't feel very good at first. Many people suggested baths as a form of relaxation so I tried that. It wasn't my cup of tea. Of course, the first time I did that I thought there was something wrong with me. Everyone else likes baths! What don't I like baths?

Then I made it *okay* for me not to like baths.

I began looking for other things. Some of them made me happy, and I enjoyed them. Others still weren't for me. But allowing myself two things made all the difference:

First, I made it a priority to look into things that made me happy. I had never been given this as a child. I wanted to find what made my soul sing. I wanted to know what I was good at, what I was a beginner at, if I had any creativity, how it would feel to have my body do certain activities. This took time too, and I still do it.

Second, I made it okay to "fail." I put this word in quotes because I don't feel they were failures now. At the time, however, it felt like failing.

I asked myself what the worst possible thing could be if I failed at what I was trying. Well, I could look like a fool. People would make fun of me. I might get physically hurt at some of them. I might lose money. I would have wasted time. And then I said that that was okay. I would still be okay if any of those things happened. But I couldn't *not* know any longer.

I had sunk as deep as I wanted to go; I wanted to know how high I could fly.

I started to find that as I was paying attention to what made me happy, what didn't feel good, and the things in my life that I *could* control, that more opportunities and more ideas for feeling good came to me! It might be an ad that I saw in a magazine, a song on the radio, a snippet of conversation overheard at the store. My perception was expanding, and I was noticing more and more amazing things coming into my experience. I thought they were coincidences; I chose to follow the ones I liked and gave myself time and space to explore them.

99% of the things I dreaded never came to pass. And when they did, I was comfortable enough with my own vulnerability that I could approach my friends or family or strangers who said something to me about their distaste of my decision. If they were open to it, I explained how my choice was making me happy. If they were not, I let them be and gave them space to process their own emotions in whatever way they chose.

Most people in our lives want us to be happy. But I have found that they do not know what makes *me* happy — only what makes *them* happy.

So I listened to what made them happy. If I wanted to, I tried it. If it didn't resonate with me, I thanked them for sharing their experience with me. They were helping me as they knew how. Ultimately, I expressed my love and support to them in whatever fashion they were willing to receive.

My desire was to *be* love.

The question I asked myself from a book I had read was "What would love do now?" Love would be and allow others to be.

A friend of mine many years ago shared something with me along this journey. She put a picture of herself as a little baby on her fridge and reminded herself that that little innocent baby is how God sees her and how we came to this world. When I wanted to beat myself up and tell myself how awful I am, I looked at a picture of me as a child buried in sand at the beach with a huge grin on my face, and I felt love for that child. I share this with you so that if it helps you when you are low, you may think of yourself as that child. After all, that child *is* you.

In the summer of 2013, I had a spiritual awakening. I understood how we are all desirous of making ourselves happy. It is what we are seeking. We are seeking pleasure, to feel joy. I was always a "bleeding heart," as some would say, but I now experienced compassion and love of myself.

I am not perfect, nor do I now desire to be. I desire to be love, and I had to learn how to do that for myself. When I could do that for myself, I did not see any separation between myself and others. We are **One**.

And it was the most beautiful life-giving experience I have ever known.

That is what I refer to as my spiritual awakening. I was in love with life, and wanted to be and share joy.

Shortly after that—in a matter of two months

actually—my ascension began. I started being contacted by spirit, and my journey continues. I am developing psychic abilities and receiving messages that blow my little human mind on a daily basis. I am so grateful to be able to be on the earth during this time, and I see so much potential, both activated and latent. I cannot imagine a more exciting time to be in 3D, and I would not miss this for anything.

I want to share one more thing: I have received this message many times, and am awed each time: *I was not supposed to wake up.* I came here for a completely different purpose. I woke up through surrender, acceptance and self-love.

My desire for you is to use what works from this piece, and leave the rest. Only *you* know what resonates with you.

You are loved. I love you. The Universe loves you. Your angels are with you right now. (They're so excited for you!)

And I wish you peace.

Namaste.

Sarah Krajewski Webb
New Jersey, USA
SarahKrajewskiWebb.com
TheOneWhoListens.com

• A LEAP OF FAITH •

THE ENERGIES OF 2013 challenged me to step out of my comfort zone and engage in Leaps of Faith.

Some leaps landed me gracefully on the other side where I gained layers of confidence and self-empowerment. Others had me crashing to the ground where I dusted myself off and climbed back up. But even those crashes created more layers of confidence and huge self-understanding.

I had one such leap and crash in 2013.

I fell hard.

Why do the big lessons always catch us slightly off guard and seem to zap us while we are down? Simply, that is how we learn the best.

We do not always pay attention otherwise. Being spiritual and psychic, as I am, does not mean life is always easy. It does mean however, that when life gets sticky and messy I have tools to deal with the energies.

As the Psychic Cowgirl, I have many opportunities fall into my path. Some are more interesting than others. Through following my spiritual guidance I found myself in a situation that had all the appearances of a great opportunity. I went into the situation excited and hopeful, and perhaps a little naive. I was imagining the promises and possibilities coming true and the success that would be headed my way. I was invested not only financially but emotionally to have this experience and expand my business.

The reality and energy of the situation began to feel less than wonderful as the final details were ironed out and the launch date of the collaboration approached. I gave it my best try. I used all my tools. I tried over and over again to relay my concerns to the parties involved. I found myself having endless conversations with trusted friends and advisers to understand what was really happening, the lessons, and how to proceed.

I began to dread the days of working on this, the sparkle and excitement was waning, and it was only the beginning of the partnership. I have realized that when I am spending hours of energy trying to figure out a situation, and no solutions show up, it may be time to let it go. That is how it works in my world. There is no benefit to a situation that is energetically draining—I had to make a change.

Honestly, I did not want to let it go. My business mind did not want to take the big financial hit. But I felt stifled, controlled, and manipulated. I had to find out the hard way. That is just how I roll. (Sound familiar?)

At 3am one morning I heard my phone ding with the note from the Universe… except my phone was set on vibrate. I said, "Hi Universe, I am concerned about a situation. Is this a heads up on the answer?" It was in that moment that I decided I'd had enough. I was giving too much energy to a situation in which the other party was not doing their part. Paying someone really well to provide a service that is not happening is no longer acceptable. If I lost the money I had invested, so be it. I was committed to a successful business partnership and I'd paid in good faith. Sometimes you simply have to know when to walk away.

I had one last business commitment to get through. EPIC FAIL on the service I had paid very well for. It was not the first time that the technical part had glitches. But now there was also an attitude about it which was unprofessional and blatantly rude to my people. It validated my decision to be done. I am super thankful for that.

I love clean energy lines, and energy does not lie. It wasn't all bad. I'd collaborated with individuals who were excellent. We'd got stuff done and worked very well together. Unfortunately, this partnership was not a fit. I cannot work successfully with energies tarnished with manipulation and pure BS. Perhaps this investment was not the best idea ever—kudos to them on excellent salespeople.

I tried my best and that is all I can do. I do not let money control my life.

Did it feel uncomfortable? Yes. Did it feel like I'd failed somehow? Yes. Did it feel like I was misguided and that my much loved and trusted spiritual team had let me down? NO, absolutely not.

I have learned in my years of being psychic that you do not get to see the big lessons coming. Big lessons are designed for soul growth and being fully immersed in the experience is part of the challenge.

I've learned that conversations on the phone can be used to manipulate and make promises that are promptly forgotten. I learned to read the fine print. I learned that a pat on the head and an "It's OK, dear, you do not know what you are talking about," can be felt as clear energetically as in person. I learned that consciousness and client care can be marketing buzzwords.

I have taken a financial hit from this experience which is frustrating considering the failure to provide the service I was paying for. There were far too many ignored e-mails, phone call appointments that were blown off, and lack of understanding for me to ever trust that situation would get better. I am too good at what I do to put up with BS that is not fertilizing my pasture.

Do I think these are bad people or that the business sucks? No. I am sure it provides a welcome service to a lot of people. I am not one of them. I am well aware that I vibrate in an energy that people cannot always understand or relate to. When I tuned into the 'behind the scenes' of the situation I realized that this business transaction was not for me.

Do I wish for an acknowledgement on the failure to provide the service I paid very well for? Of course.

Do I wish I could get my money back? Of course.

Did I walk away knowing that they do not roll that way? Of course.

I do wish them the best of luck in their future endeavors. To be clear, I left this situation because the energy being created is not in alignment with Psychic Cowgirl, and I have the power and freedom of choice. I am very grateful for the experience I am a much better person for it.

Shannon Laackmann
The Psychic Cowgirl
Alberta, Canada
PsychicCowgirl.com

• EXPECTATIONS AND FEARS •

2013 WAS A YEAR of great challenges and huge personal growth for me.

It started in Alaska where I was having depression and anxiety from the winters. I had struggled with anxiety for years, but it had changed from panic attacks to a full-blown anxiety disorder. I had lived in Alaska seven years and was being guided by the fairies to move. It seemed like a daunting task, but I knew my time in the arctic was done. I put in my work transfer to Seattle and packed my belongings.

After moving, I expected to feel better right away, but was discouraged it didn't happen. I knew the fairies were helping me—they left me signs by guiding me to meet musicians and fairy artists. They also guided me through an oracle deck to become vegan! This was something I wouldn't have considered, but every time I did a reading for myself, the card came up. One of my friends in Alaska was guided to pull a card for me and it was the same one. I started cutting back on meat in August and, although it was challenging, it gave me a sense of peace. I spoke to the fairies out loud in my apartment one night about becoming vegan and one manifested! I knew what I was seeing was real because my cat saw her too! I knew I was on the right track.

In October, I had a week of vacation. Money had been very tight since the move, however, I felt guided to visit Sedona, Arizona. I gave myself a fairy card reading and it supported my feeling by telling me to visit a spiritual power place. I asked why and it said for healing. This was validated by Archangel Michael in a separate reading. I was also guided to start posting my experiences on Twitter!

Before I went to Sedona, I spent the night in Flagstaff, Arizona. There, I had a vision of hands with healing energy coming off them, and a second vision of a fairy crown with blue-green metallic energy coming off it! I've had visions before, but never in metallic colors!

The next day in Sedona was wonderful: a vortex tour, shopping, and good food. I felt a bit confused, however, because I expected more. I didn't feel much at all from the vortexes. It wasn't until the next night, at my parent's home in Nevada, that I had a vision of ten or twenty metallic pink fairy lights as I was drifting off to sleep! This started a massive amount of healing and growth.

So much happened in the last two months of the year that I was racing to keep up with it all!

My spiritual gifts were developing rapidly, however, I realized I had very deep fear blocks. I couldn't figure out where they came from. It's normal to have fear based on past experiences, but this seemed unnatural. It was extremely difficult to admit to myself I didn't trust anyone—not the fairies, angels, Spirit, myself, or other people.

Where was this coming from?

I wanted to connect to the angels and fairies so badly in more than just card readings, but I was terrified.

I met a psychic woman who explained I had been deeply betrayed by someone in a past life—to the point they had taken my life. She apologized to me on their behalf and I felt cleansing, healing energy wash over me! It was as though a huge weight was lifted from me!

I also met a woman online who channels archangels and received a message from

Archangel Michael! He told me he wanted to help me release my fear blocks and that he had agreed to be my guardian angel before I was born!

I started visualizing blowing my fears into my cupped hands and when I couldn't anymore, I would hand them to Archangel Michael. I asked him to take them to the light and transform them into Love for me. He actually appeared in my mind's eye once while I was handing my fears to him! He was floating above me, smiling lovingly at me.

I began feeling better, but knew I had a lot more healing work to do.

Several weeks later I found myself deeply drawn to an apophyllite crystal in a spiritual store in Honolulu, Hawaii. I felt the angels telling me to hold it in my hands. When I did, I was overwhelmed by the energy. I felt intense Love from Spirit and the angels. I was moved to tears because I hadn't felt energy that strong from a crystal before.

I took her home with me and started meditating with her. I started seeing energy from several of my chakras one night, and was alarmed when I was shown my root chakra. It was almost completely black with two pin pricks of red light. The angels showed me this twice because I didn't realize at first it was my root chakra. I asked Archangels Raphael and Michael to cleanse and balance my chakras. They were healing me in my sleep, and I was surprised to see the golden energy of Jesus appear, too.

I asked them to work with me every night for several weeks. I saw my chakra once more about halfway through the healing sessions. I saw the progress that was made so far. It still had black on it, but less of it, and the red was bright metallic!

I felt the exact moment my chakras became balanced and healthy. I was driving to see a therapist about my anxiety and I realized why I came to earth was to learn about the illusion of fear! I was meant to have these challenges in order to help people.

To learn about fear is to learn about Love. I felt a deep peace, something I had never felt before in my life.

I remembered a dream I had the night before that Archangel Michael and I were channeling energy from heaven to earth together. I'm not sure how this will manifest, yet, but I know it is no coincidence that I've experienced so many fears, and that archangel Michael is with me.

I went from deep depression and anxiety to Spirit lifting me up through beings of Love!

I am so blessed to experience my spiritual awakening when I need it most! I don't know what I'll be called to do in the future, but I really

look forward to finding out.
Love and bright blessings to you!

Nikki Beard
Seattle, Washington, USA
Twitter: @nikkialaina

• SPREADING CALM •

My NAME IS GARY Molloy, and I spent 10 years in and out of hospital in London, suffering severe episodes of Bipolar Disorder.

I Finally came out of the Nightmare in march 2000 and made a pledge to myself that I would do all in my power to find ways, means, and everything possible to no longer end up in hospital, sometimes for months at a time.

The first thing I did was quit Alcohol and found Art as a way of Channeling the crippling mood swings. I have been learning to manage and this march will celebrate 14 years not having had an admission to hospital.

In 2009, I got help to publish my first book, *The Storm before the Calm*, a book mainly of oil paintings and a little of the recovery story.

2013 was a very positive year, and I feel I have grown and the healing process in my life is gaining momentum.

In June 2013, I was an influential part of the British Charity Mind's campaign to End the Restraint Technique in Mental Hospitals in the UK. I had been restrained many times when the mania was extreme and it is the most frightening and degrading thing that can happen to anyone. Since I was last in Hospital in 2000, there have been 13 deaths from the use of this method, sometimes by inexperienced nurses.

The campaign I had a major part in is now close to having the law changed in the UK, and I was lucky to go to the Houses of Parliament and discuss this with MP's as well as other mental health issues.

I have also worked as a volunteer for Bipolar UK for 8 years, and in 2013 got the chance to help many Sufferers and their families by sharing advice and support on all aspects of recovery.

In 2013, my poetry was published, and I had a couple of group exhibitions in London; the theme was mainly to break down the terrible Stigma that still exists within mental health in the UK.

Finally, as the year 2013 was drawing to a close, a program I made with Kerry Katona, who is a singer here in the UK, was broadcast on national TV, and the feedback was very positive, with many saying it has helped them greatly to understand Bipolar.

My Goal is to continue to help, encourage, and hopefully inspire people to break free from any type of mental anguish, and to find a more peaceful and calm way to live.

Gary Molloy
London, UK
GaryMolloy.blogspot.com

• PERCEPTIONS •

2013 HAS OFFERED ME a multitude of opportunities for learning and growth, in more ways than one.

I finally attained the courage to self-publish not one, but three books this year. I finished writing *Journey into Consciousness,* and submitted the manuscript to publishers in October 2012. My perception has always been that I needed a publisher in order to be considered a credible writer. I received a few responses, indicating my submission "didn't fit their categories" or was "too autobiographical." After apologizing for the delay in responding because of the hundreds of submissions they receive, one publishing company wrote:

> "...*unfortunately, the majority are the same type as yours: an autobiography of how someone found their path of spirituality. We have found that these do not sell well, unless they have a unique twist, but it does show how humanity is awakening and becoming aware of their abilities.*"

So, I just set the manuscript aside and waited.

In February 2013, I had the honor of being asked by *OMTimes Magazine* to write a tribute article for spiritual luminary Debbie Ford.

As soon as I submitted the article, my guides came through and asked me, "Are you credible now? They asked you to write. You are a writer." This interaction with my guides immediately shifted my perception. They then instructed me to revisit, revise and refresh my two *DailyOM* courses, *Stop Existing and Start Living!* and *Opening Your Heart to Love,* and publish them as books. Their reasoning is that courses have the feel of obligation and responsibility, and some people are just not ready for that commitment. A book can simply be read. Thus, my two books, *28 Days to a New YOU* and *Connect to the YOU Within* were birthed in the spring of 2013, with the creative assistance of Lloyd Matthew Thompson of *Starfield Press.*

Shifting my perception, I freed myself from those self-imposed limitations and the outdated (old paradigm) way of thinking. As an intuitive medium, Reiki Master, spiritual teacher, and now, book author, I was able to find the peace and ability to be comfortable with who I am and how I work, specifically in regards to delivering messages in group settings. I feel like I am able to fully allow myself to release the fear of what other people will think or say about me, or the work I do. I realize that I can't please everyone, but I can please myself. Cue the music—can you hear the song playing now?

The way I read, heal, teach, etc. is unique to me because *I* am unique, and I should not question it or compare myself or my journey to another.

This year has also allowed me the ability to really see everyone and everything as well as every experience through the eyes of love. Each one of us are at different places on our life journey, and we should never compare our intended life experiences to another person's journey.

Whether I am interacting with another individual, or offering guidance to others, I love each person individually, and "see" them where they are at that moment, while recognizing that the choices they make are "right" for them. Who am I to say otherwise? By honoring who I am and the journey that we are each on, I have freed myself from the self-imposed restraints of those energetic shackles.

I opted to move forward and publish *Journey into Consciousness* in October 2013. I decided to revisit what I had previously written and immediately acknowledged how much I had grown in the past year. After editing what I had written by deleting parts and inserting new experiences, *Journey into Consciousness* was released December 2, 2013.

This book may revolve around my story, but within each one of us is a story that is being written each and every day. We are constantly writing the story of our lives based on choices — whether we make these choices ourselves or they are made for us. The directions those choices take us form the foundation for our learning, spiritual growth, and even our happiness. From the moment we breathe that first breath of life to the moment that final breath exits our body, our life story is being written. As we become more aware and mindful of our own personal power, we are better able to make conscious choices, and give ourselves permission to take control of our destiny instead of leaving it up to fate.

Over the years, I've learned that letting go of fear is a crucial part of spiritual growth, and as a human being, I know that fear is what has held me back and inhibited my ability to write this book for a long time. My personal fears about this recounting of my personal journey into consciousness revolve around the uncertainty of what is safe to share: What will my parents think? What will my husband think? What will my children think? Just how much is enough? As Spirit pushed me to begin writing, I kept coming up with every excuse as to why I should not write this book. The fear became especially strong as it became very clear to me that Spirit wanted—no, expected—me to share everything that I did.

I acknowledge that the memories of my experiences are solely my perception—my viewpoint.

As I tell my story, I do so with the intention of assisting others in awakening to the truth of who they really are and to help them live the life they desire. I apologize if I inadvertently cause anyone hurt or pain, but my memories are crucial to the telling of my story, and it was Spirit who showed me which memories to share.

When I asked for guidance on this front, in an instant, a rush of memories flooded me—one right after the other. I realized that they were showing me what I needed to share, what mattered, what was important. The memories I was shown are the pivotal ones that impacted me greatly in my early years. I was shown the memories and choices that molded and shaped me—creating who I am today.

My primary objectives for writing the book are as follows:

1) To assist in bringing an understanding of

one's life experiences and the consequences of choices made without blaming others

2) To learn to heal from the past through forgiveness and shifting perception

3) To allow ourselves to realize our full potential through empowerment and love

The night before the book was released, I began to feel extremely vulnerable as I realized many people would be reading the story of my spiritual awakening. I wasn't afraid or nervous, I simply felt vulnerable and exposed.

Just when I thought the year was a smooth and easy one relatively speaking, 2013's real lesson was presented to me the last week of 2013.

On December 29, 2013, I received a one-star review on my book, *Journey into Consciousness*, on Amazon.com. The review itself wasn't "bad" per se, and I allowed myself to receive the constructive criticism as it was intended. The reviewer opted to compare my book to another that she preferred. She noted, *"P.S. And since Shelly is so spiritually enlightened, I know that she will just recognize me as a messenger."* Indeed, I did!

I immediately viewed her as the messenger and promptly contacted the author of the book mentioned, and she will be joining me for a conversation on my Blog Talk Radio Show. Little did I know the role this review would play in the next few days.

On December 31, 2013, my mom called me at an inopportune time to discuss my book that she chose to purchase on her own. I made the conscious choice early on not to give her one as her beliefs differed from my own. On more than one occasion, she made it very clear, that she didn't agree or even like the work I do. During the phone call, she very angrily communicated her displeasure with what I had written and said "You are a liar, delusional, and have a mental illness." I told her they were my memories and the perception of my experiences, and she replied, "No, you are just a liar who needs help."

Lots more words were uttered, and I found myself in a foggy daze trying to make sense of what I was hearing. I said very little and just listened without reacting. She obviously pushed my buttons, triggering something deep within me, and she intended to. I was emotionally and physically drained from the short conversation, yet chose to see this experience from the Higher soul perspective. I recognized there was a reason this conversation happened on the last day of the year.

On a bright note, I called my dad afterwards, who I actually gave a copy to, and asked for his thoughts. He said he had just finished it and shared honestly his impressions. His reaction was at the opposite end of the spectrum. He acknowledged that what I shared was truth and also made a point to let me know how he remembered certain experiences. The manner in which he conveyed them to me was not one of judgment, but compassion and consolation. He let me know that he recognizes how perception, which is how we view our experiences, will alter the memory itself.

He told me that he initially started to read excerpts from the book and was upset. He decided to honor me, my story, and the book by investing the time to read it cover to cover. He is thankful that he did and then said he still isn't sure about the mediumship part. He stated that while he was reading the book the day before, the television was on and *The Steve Harvey Show* came on. Steve's guest just happened to be the Long Island Medium Teresa Caputo. Dad watched the show and was enamored. I definitely thank Spirit for the synchronicity!

The next day, I found out that my mom had printed off the one-star review and gave it to my sister-in-law to give to my brother to read. Perhaps, this was her way of validating her own impression. I'm not sure to be honest. A former friend/colleague also opted to share his comments on the review as well.

With that being said, I made the conscious choice to honor myself and what I was feeling. I cried for hours that evening releasing the pain my mother's words inflicted on me. Rather than trying to figure out why this was happening now at this time, I chose to see this experience as one of healing, clearing and growth. Consciously, I feared what she would think when she read it, but I chose not to go there with her. Spirit made sure that I did go there, and blessed me with a beautiful and healing conversation with my dad.

Reflecting on your own life experiences, I encourage you to acknowledge your experiences, whether you deem them pleasant or unpleasant, as opportunities for learning and growth. These experiences do not define you, but will undoubtedly have an impact on who you are today.

As a spiritual teacher, I wish to reiterate the importance of seeing things from a Higher perspective—your soul's perspective. Your soul chose to incarnate to Earth school for this lifetime. Your soul chose opportunities for learning and growth. While your human-ness doesn't remember and cannot understand these challenges, your soul understands. Seeing things from the Higher perspective, each one of us are expressions of Source consciousness/God. We are having this human life experience as us (who we chose to be incarnated as during this lifetime) to learn, grow, and evolve.

When presented with challenges, I encourage you to pause, step back, *breathe*, and then allow yourself the opportunity to choose how you wish to react.

In the big scheme of things, there are five things you can control. You have control of your thoughts, words, actions, emotions, and reactions. Everything else is beyond your control. You can choose how you wish to react, and sometimes the appropriate response is to have no reaction at all.

Take a moment to breathe in deeply and let go of the lower vibration emotions of fear, worry, doubt, regret, guilt, shame, anger, frustration, etc. and breathe in the higher vibration of love. Focus your energy on this present moment, and allow yourself to be embraced in the loving embrace of the Divine.

Allow yourself to acknowledge these experiences, express your gratitude with sincerity for having them, and then honor yourself by moving forward with grace and ease. There is nothing to be gained by blaming anyone for your life's experiences. Take ownership of them and see the blessings within the challenges. When you do, you will shift the energy of those experiences. The more that you allow yourself the opportunity to live in the moment by bringing all of your energy to the here and now rather than dwelling in the past or contemplating the future, the more at peace you will be. By doing so, you will also be in the flow to manifest your heart's desire.

I wish you peace. I wish you love. I wish you joy. I wish you happiness.

Shelly Wilson
Oklahoma, USA
ShellyRWilson.com
Journey-into-Consciousness.com

• DECISIONS •

IT MAY HAVE STARTED out as any other year would have, with the clock ticking to the stroke of midnight, the celebrations of fireworks in the streets, cheering, dancing, and of course, kissing. But I knew it would be far different from any other year I had yet to experience.

I was right. I could feel the change happening.

I had been in the Oil and Gas industry of Oklahoma for eight years at that point, and had worked my way up the corporate ladder in a world of fierce competition. I was good at my job, but I could see that the end was near, and there was nothing I could do about it.

Call it destiny, or what have you, but I knew it was written in the stars, I saw it in my astrology chart and I could feel the pull — the pull to get out of the corporate world and start my own thing.

So, when the work slowed down, I would go into the office every day and wonder if today was the day that I wouldn't have anything left to do.

That day came at the end of March. I finished up the project I was working on and there was nothing left for me to do. Even my boss didn't have anything to do. The project had ended, and there was not another one waiting.

My old, egoic self would have been terrified, but my new, more spiritually centered self was ecstatic at the potential freedom, and couldn't wait to see what magical things were about to happen.

Okay, I admit, I was just a little freaked out. Only a little. I had a month's worth of income that was going to be coming in from the Oil and Gas job, and I knew I had a month to essentially get my shit together.

This was the point of do-or-die. I didn't want to go back to another desk job where I was put in the corner and punished for being social. I wanted to break free from being questioned on where I was going every time I left my desk. It was incredibly annoying. I mean, can't a girl pee in peace? This was my chance to make a run for it!

Up to that point I had been working on building my online raw food coaching business at

TheNewRawYou.com. I loved the idea of being able to make a life and living for myself through something I was passionate about.

A few months before this point one of my raw food coaching clients found out that I had years of office experience with the main core being database management. She saw how I had been able to build my online business through translating the skills I had learned from the office and applying them to the online world. She needed help with her website and asked me to help her with it and to become her Virtual Assistant (VA for short).

She was asking me to help her do something I loved doing and was going to pay me for it? How could I refuse? I couldn't!

I instantly said yes, and got a taste for what being a VA was all about. So, when my office job ended, I knew I could take my skills to other online business owners to gain more clients as a Virtual Assistant. And that's exactly what I did.

I had a month to hustle — and boy did I hustle!

I had my one and only client help by recommending me to people she knew could use my help and I applied for a few positions I came across on websites as well.

Then one day I got an email from a list I was on from a guy I was following who was asking for people to join his team. He needed more support staff members and turned it into a contest by asking for potential applicants to send in a short video answering a few specific questions. I figured why the heck not and did it.

I got the job!

Then I had this thought that I needed to contact a person I had recently met about helping him with a potential business that I had helped him dream up. I was nervous about it, fought it for a few days then talked to my boyfriend, Lee, about it. He had been having the same inclination as I had been about the same person as well. I took that as a sign and figured why the heck not about that, too, and did it—it was a risk I had to do.

It took a few days before I heard back from him and guess what? He was overjoyed that I had contacted him! Then he proceeded to tell me he had sold the idea to another business partner of his, but had taken my offer to another close friend of his who needed help putting a large book project together and said he would be contacting me soon about it.

I knew the name of his friend from somewhere, but couldn't quite put my finger on it.

Within a half hour his friend messaged me on Facebook, and after talking to him for a few minutes I realized where I recognized his name from. I was on his list and had been following him for a while. This guy was kind of a big deal.

I couldn't help smiling a huge shit-eating grin for hours. My intuition was right. Lee's intuition was right. I was living and embracing the law of attraction more and more every day. This was good stuff!

I gained a few smaller clients, and within two months I was making enough to keep me afloat financially. I was able to pay all of my bills and live in more alignment with my spirit and path.

I was ecstatic!

I woke up every day to a life I loved, next to my soulmate and twin flame, working with passion for people who quickly became my dear friends and colleagues, teaching me what I needed to learn as I grew as a person and their businesses all at the same time. Plus, I got to express my creativity as I did it all.

Then Lee proposed to me, right in the middle of our shared home office. It couldn't have been more perfect. (Of course I said yes!)

During all of this I was legally liable under the terms of my divorce from my ex-husband to refinance the house or sell it. After getting back my credit report and finding out that my ex had tanked my credit score because he hadn't made the payments on time on a truck we had co-signed on together right before he traded it in, I got the message loud and clear. I knew I had to sell the house. I had been feeling the pull from spirit to move, but some things are harder for me to let go of than others. My beloved house in Oklahoma was one of those things.

Lee runs an online business for a guy who is based in Atlanta, Georgia, and wanted to open up an office so he could grow the business and eventually either get investors for it or sell it. Lee needed to be in Atlanta since he runs it all.

That would mean that I would need to move to Atlanta as well.

Since I had already been feeling the pull to move, I could see where spirit was leading me. I had to sell my house due to things beyond my control and had someone offering to pay for moving expenses. It was obvious.

The only catch was my two boys. My ex-husband wasn't going to go for being separated from them, and my oldest son already lived with him full time by choice. That left the youngest one as the main consideration.

This ate at me for months and months and I delayed it as long as possible. I consulted with friends and family and Lee. I was beside myself with the torment of what the possibilities were. I knew it could go either way, but when I would see my boys with their daddy, it broke my heart to tear them apart more than it hurt to think of not having them in my life everyday.

I finally had to let the torment go and leave it in the hands of spirit to do what was best for all involved. I had to really trust in it.

I resolved to not mention anything to my ex about the potential move until I had put the house up on the market and had it under contract. I put the house up the middle of July. It went under contract two weeks later, and I had thirty days to pack it all up and get ready to leave.

Oh, and tell my ex about it all.

Ugh!

After a lot of deep breaths, and a few days of delaying the inevitable, I finally broke the news to him.

Thankfully it went better than expected! We were able to talk about it as adults, but it was very emotional. He cried at the idea of being separated from his boys, and at the other possibility of them being separated from me. He himself growing up without a mother knew at the core how much pain it had caused him over the years.

This was not going to be an easy decision.

The next day my ex called me to tell me that he had hired an attorney as was not going to let me take the boys with me and would fight me every step of the way.

I didn't want to fight, and I didn't want to hurt about this anymore.

After a few more days weighing the most difficult decision I had ever had to make, I waived my white flag to stop the pain, and told him he had won.

I felt a great sense of relief after that, and knew I had made the right decision for the time being. Everyone in my life supported me in that decision as well.

Preparing for the upcoming move, I found an apartment north of Atlanta in Marietta, and secured it. Sight unseen. Risky? Yes, but I was short on time, and the price was right. So, I did it.

The week of the closing, Lee had to put his Jeep in the shop to get something in the motor fixed. A cracked head or something like that. Something important enough that needed to get fixed before we started traveling half way across the country, hauling stuff in it.

On the day of the closing, his Jeep still wasn't ready. We had to pack two Jeep's worth of things, plus a trailer, all into and attached to my Jeep. It was a very, very tight fit, but we made it work. I had to drive slowly so the back tires wouldn't rub when it bounced across a bump in the road.

The rest of the stuff went into a PODS container, and was picked up and would be ready for delivery once we got to Atlanta.

Until then, we had ten days of being homeless before our new apartment was going to be ready for us to move into.

Two of those days were spent waiting for Lee's Jeep. It was finally ready on Saturday morning. We went to the shop, picked it up, moved half of the stuff over from my Jeep into his and by noon we had kissed the boys goodbye, and were on the road, ready to see what was going to happen next. Dog included.

We went from Oklahoma City all the way to a KOA campground right outside of Ft. Smith, Arkansas, where we set up camp, turned on the mobile wireless internet devise, plugged our laptops into the campground plug, and worked for a little bit.

One of the great things about working online is you really can work from anywhere you have internet — even from a KOA campground in the middle of Arkansas.

Our next stop was at a friend's house in Nashville, Tennessee. From there, we headed to Atlanta, and through Atlanta to another KOA campground an hour south of the city. You could literally throw a stone and hit the highway from that one, which made it hard to sleep at night from all of the traffic. We left the next day and headed to another KOA campground in Savannah, Georgia — a place I had always dreamed of visiting.

We had a beautiful tour of the city, and stayed for two nights. It was wonderful! We then had the invitation to stay at a friend's family property for a few nights at a cabin in the mountains in north Georgia.

For 3 days and nights, we slept in a real bed in

a picturesque cabin nestled in the woods. I had found my new writing haven. It was only an hour north of Atlanta, which made it perfect for weekend getaways.

When our apartment was ready, we left the solitude of the woods and headed to the busiest and most crowded city I have ever lived in. My life has been filled with so many synchronicities and confirmations since doing so, through the people I have met and the places I have been. In doing this, I have given the opportunity to get to know and heal myself in deeper ways than I ever thought possible.

I realize that the move to Atlanta was because of Lee, but in reality we all know that this move was really meant for me, for whatever reasons the universe might have.

I know my path has led me here, and I know I did the right thing. Everyday is an exciting adventure that I get to explore. From this, I know I am safe and the Universe has my back.

Natalie Wheeler
Georgia, USA
TheNewRawYou.com

• REACHING FARTHER •

IT WAS INDEED SUCH a transformational year for me in 2013: I brought in the New Year with my children, and for the first time in a long time, with a lot of inner peace.

I could feel that things were going to shift and change, but really had no idea just *how* much.

At the beginning of the year, I chose to embark on a global fundraising mission, and joined the *Off the Mat Into the World* Global Seva Challenge. This was to be the first time that I decided to really dive head first into fundraising that had more to do with my efforts having a positive effect on the whole world, instead of my own intimate world of Multiple Sclerosis.

For the past eleven years, I've been

successfully raising money and awareness of MS, and with those funds, providing home health aide care to those who need it. While that is still very much a passion of mine, something inside of me felt that I can take what I do and help others outside of something so personal to me. Being an advocate to others and someone who literally gives her all to help others, I've never really embarked on something bigger than what effected me personally, and with this Global Seva (selfless act) Challenge, it's helped me to see the big picture—how precious our rainforests are, and how connected each of us are, no matter the circumstances.

This challenge was not met without pushback, as many don't understand why I branched out from MS into something that many are just not familiar with. However, I really do feel that it's all connected, as we all are.

There was a goal for each of us to raise twenty thousand dollars, and if that was done, we got to go with my mentor, Seane Corn, to Ecuador and see how and what our fundraising efforts were being put to use for.

My goal was very different; it was really to help bring out the awareness of the danger our rainforests are in, and how that if we don't protect them and care for our earth, the "lungs of the earth" were being compromised. My goal was to be part of something so much bigger than myself, and although I came nowhere near the goal of twenty thousand dollars, I did raise nearly one thousand dollars, and the reward for me was actually being part of this beautiful *Sangha* (family, community) of like-minded people who are all doing something good that affects every one of us around the world.

I consciously chose to take my yoga practice off the mat and into the world, even more so than I'd been doing for the past eleven years. I learned so much from this experience, and also realized that I need to figure out how to maintain my support of raising money and awareness for MS, but also take that drive I have and enable myself to do good for the *greater* good, without draining or compromising myself and my energy — something I'm still working on.

As the year moved forward, I also chose to commit to teaching my free yoga for MS classes in a yoga studio for the first time, and then committed to continue teaching these classes after our program ended, even though I still don't get paid to do this. I really discovered that my purpose in life is to teach and to bring this gift of yoga to as many people who are living with not only MS, but any invisible chronic illness. By bringing the gift of yoga to as many people as possible, my hope is that others will discover, like I did some nine years ago, that we are so much more capable than we think, and *can* do so much more, if just given the opportunity and safety to. This is what I am so blessed to bring to my classes.

I had such an amazing year—I even got scholarships to attend the Yoga Journal Conference in New York City, which I truly believe helped catapult me into understanding that MS was and is my divine assignment! I am meant to be living in this body, with this disease, and to experience what it is I do experience, so that I can teach and help others like myself, or others who are living with a like challenge.

I've gotten to study with some of my favorite teachers, and each experience just seamlessly opened doors to the next. From the Yoga Journal Conference to going to Wanderlust Vermont and practicing with some of the worlds best teachers, to finding out how much my body could do when I simply make a choice to live my very best life in this body, whether she feels good or not—but always mindful of the gift of determination and strength I am blessed with.

I learned that all of life is a choice, and my yoga practice really became such a way of life, more so than ever before. I even got the amazing blessing to be part of a group of assistants to volunteer and assist Seane Corn as she taught over a thousand people down by the Brooklyn Bridge in the fall! To look out at the huge park full of like-minded people who were all there to simply be together as One with their mind, body, and soul was a gift and experience that I was so grateful to be a part of.

This past year my children all reached milestone birthdays, from my oldest turning 21 to my youngest turning 16, and my middle daughter turning 18. There were many moments within my family life that really had lessons to teach me as well.

My son was going through and is still going through some really hard times, and I had to learn to parent with tough love—something I'm still working on. It's not easy to watch our children or our young adults stand on the train tracks with the train coming right at them, knowing, and yet not having any way to "control" the situation or save them. I found out that sometimes as parents we really do have to "Let go, and let God." Our children are on their own journeys, and sometimes love means saying no, even when saying no hurts. I have had to learn that we can't save them, but can only guide them. The same way I've learned through my own life lessons—mistakes and all—will be the same way they do. It's so hard as a parent to let go, but it's so necessary for their own growth to do so.

This was the hardest part of this past year, and it continues to be something I'm still struggling with, but I'm also at peace knowing that one day, he will understand that everything I did or didn't do was out of love.

I was also blessed to meet Marianne Williamson, and she really helped me to understand that no parent gets away without some kind of parent guilt, and although I feel that guilt is a useless emotion, it's one that I experienced the moment I realized that with all of my strength, determination, and "I've got this" momentum that my son has watched was really me living in the feminine, but carrying a lot of masculine energy, which in essence confused him and caused him to react towards me in the mirror image of what he saw.

What a huge wake up call!

I never realized that being strong and self-sufficient for ourselves and our children, despite how we might really be feeling can send off a message of "I don't need anyone's help."

Really understanding the feminine/masculine aspects of myself and others has helped me a great deal in learning how to speak to my son in a way he might understand, and has also helped me to stop allowing myself to be a doormat, keeping in mind what Marianne explained about how love sometimes says no.

This past year I celebrated my eleventh anniversary of living with Multiple Sclerosis, and really understood what a blessing being diagnosed with this disease has been and continues to be.

I've always been the type of person who wants to help others. However, I am not sure who I would have become if I hadn't been diagnosed with MS. I'm not sure I would have found yoga or become a yoga teacher, and I know that if none of those things happened, I'd never have had the opportunity to help so many people from this amazing place of knowing and understanding.

Besides my own family issues, I also lost a friend to complications of an MS Treatment, and realized just how lucky I was to have chosen to go off that very same treatment when I did, or else I might have met with the same fate. I realize that being an advocate for ourselves is so important, but not only for ourselves — as Maya Angelou says, "When you learn, teach." We are shown and experience things every day, not just to keep for ourselves, but to give away. To appreciate every moment, it's the only moment we truly have.

2013 was such a wakeup call on so many levels, from how precious life is and how we really only have control of two things: how we prepare for things, and how we react when and if something happens.

Life is so much about balance and awareness.

This year, I really discovered both.

I was blessed with the most incredible

experiences, and at the same time had to deal with challenges that every time it seemed as if my life was going on track, there were suddenly stumbling blocks in my path — then I learned that the blocks were there to learn from; they remind us to pause, and slow down.

I've learned true forgiveness, forgiving myself and others, and letting go of any grudges or harsh feelings for people that I felt did me wrong.

In actuality, those things that I labeled wrong were really all part of my lessons, and they've helped me to become a better person. There really is no separation between me and anyone — we are all connected, and everything we do has an effect on someone else, whether we are aware of it or not. There is really a ripple effect, and it's powerful. It's so important to be mindful of our words and actions, to pause, to love, and to come from love and let go of fear. This was and still is my biggest lesson I'm still working on. Letting go of the fears — whatever they might be — and trusting: trusting the process, trusting that everything at every moment is happening exactly as it's supposed to, and even if I can't see clearly why something is happening, there most certainly is a divine reason it is. It's amazing to me when we let go of the control knobs and just allow. All is eventually revealed to us.

I am blogging and writing more than ever, and I am finally working on putting together my book. I feel I have so much to share, so many positive life experiences. Some were absolutely painful, but at the end of the day have made me the person that I am today and continue to grow to be. I am hopeful that my book will inspire others to live well, no matter what life throws at them, and to never give up.

I have realized that I can practice yoga for the rest of my life, and even teach yoga for that long, too! It will *always* amaze and humble me to remember, that when I allow life and external circumstances to disturb my inner peace, that the way back home to my center is my practice. Even though sometimes it takes me a minute or longer to remember, I *do* remember, and I return to what I know is my center, to the quiet of my mind, the company of my breath, my moving and sometimes not-moving meditation, and there I release anything that no longer serves me.

What a gift one can give to their soul!

I'm so grateful, and gratitude has really been my greatest lesson of 2013. I am taking that into 2014 and beyond.

Lisa Bachrach-Zeankowski
Hicksville, NY
LisaBachrach.com

• FIRSTHAND DARKNESS •

IT WAS IN THE year of two thousand thirteen that darkness touched me, firsthand.

It was then I realized just how deep a darkness people are capable of.

Before 2013, sure, I saw how awful this place could be, how downright horrible and devastating. But even then, they were really just stories; I still held the highest faith in people. I stubbornly insisted that people were inherently good; that above all, people would always choose the best for everyone involved—Grinches with bejeweled hearts secreted away.

I probably even imagined them taking out those precious hearts, and enjoying them behind the safety of closed doors—they just didn't want anyone to know about it, right? Bullies are supposed to really be teddy bears, once you get to know them.

I *know* I trusted they would act from this space of kindness at the end of the day, when things came down to the wire.

But I had not yet been put to the personal test of experiencing such things in my own life.

What I should clearly have known—what movies and stories endlessly attempt to portray to us—is that the "bad guys" are bad guys for a reason, and will most likely remain the bad guys, defiant and insistent on it to their very end, spitting curses at the hero as their very body dissolves into a gulf of flames.

I discovered that Grinches, with all their heart-growing-at-the-end-of-the-episode, seem to be the exception, not the rule.

But that is not really the point of my story here.

It is easy to accept the fact that there will always be hateful people. It's easy to voice that you know there will always be somebody trying to weasel anything free out of anyone they can; that there will always be those who will not bat an eyelash at harming others physically, emotionally, or spiritually, if they believe it will gain themselves something—even if those others are their own families and children.

It is also easy to read and study and fancy yourself "practicing" a higher set of standards, telling yourself you are living by them, when in reality all you've done is *imagine* them — imagine what you would do *if* certain situations came to your life.

When the reality of those certain situations — at times very difficult and impossible situations — hit you for real, *as* real, it is then that you discover exactly what your true colors are. You begin to see what you really have inside.

And I found my natural response to hatefulness was... hate.

Anger.

Irrational ranting and plotting.

Where did that come from?

How did I drop so quickly to *that?*

Twelve years of meditation, studying, and patterning myself to make sure I was a gentle, compassionate, and unconditionally loving person were instantly overridden by an emotional, chemical, and primal nature the moment my family and myself was threatened.

It is extremely difficult to maintain the view that certain people are "simply hurting and hopeless, and just need more love shown to them" when they are stomping on your face and holding your most precious treasures hostage for the sole purposes of controlling you or getting something they want from you.

And I feel that in 2013 I truly *real*-ized: until one has come face to face with an experience of something, and has gone through it directly, one cannot know how one will react in a given situation. One cannot know what one is talking about. One cannot claim to be an expert at it. One may have the knowledge of and historical facts on the best and worst ways to handle a thing, but until they have been tried, tested, and *burned* by that thing, one simply *does not know*.

You see yourself in a whole new light when you reach this point. You come to the crossroads of deciding you've wasted your time for years and should throw it all away, since bullies and manipulators seem to always get their way without consequences anyway, or to continue believing that although the world is full of spew, every ounce of light beamed from even the most insignificant of people *does* make a difference, gather your resolve, and transmute the crap into fuel to spur even greater feats of strength, untouched.

So now that I know, and now that I see… which do I choose?

In sitting with the pain…

In sitting with the character I wish to embody, and have worked so diligently to become…

I strip away each, and frantically search for what rests at my core.

And I find…

All the work I've done for thirty-five years has been able to *be* done because it is *who I am*.

It is what I always return to, always bounce back to, no matter what, *because* it is what I am.

I find an incredible peace in honestly and nakedly discovering that it is no act put on for my readers, no show performed for the clients I heal, no ruse to *pretend* I am a good person—I truly am… this.

I choose to carry on.

Am I stronger now, thanks to 2013?

Surely I must be.

I know myself—my dark *and* my light—better than I ever have before, because of these experiences.

Is that then the purpose of "bad guys" in the world, these people spewing and vomiting filth on this otherwise amazing planet?

Are they here for more than the vague textbook answer of "to bring balance" and be the dark's opposite to the light?

Do they volunteer and choose to come be nasties here, so that those truly aspiring toward higher realms will have catapults for their ascensions?

If this is so, it would mean that the "hatefuls" are the most benevolent *Bodhisattvas* in the world—those holy beings who willingly stay behind to assist others in growing ahead. Now isn't *that* a trip to consider…

Lloyd Matthew Thompson
Oklahoma, USA
GalaxyEnergy.org

• THE VENUS-PLUTO CYCLE •

I GOT INTO ASTROLOGY in a big way in 2013, not realizing at the time how much of an impact it was going to have on my life—the planetary aspects, not the research.

It seems that the biggest changes in my life this past year have centered on relationships—the breakdown of my marriage especially—and these have coincided with the Venus-Pluto cycle, and the eclipse cycle.

Ironically, in January, I didn't even realize that my marriage was no longer working, despite all the obvious signs. In my eyes, and I think my husband's eyes, we had a comfortable marriage in which we were more friends than ardent lovers, but it worked for us, and enabled us to raise our children, who were 8 and 5 at the time. We'd also been married for 16 years, and who expects passion after such a long marriage anyway?

We had first met through a dating service at the end of 1992, before dating services went online. After three years of living together, we got married in 1996. We were both technology workers and computer gamers, and had no plans on having children. Well, times change, we closed our company shortly after the dot-com crash, and while Jason managed to get his old job back disgustingly easily, I remained unemployed as the demand for web designers was rapidly being outsourced to India.

Left at home alone, I dabbled in being a housewife, got my real estate license and discovered just how much hormones can alter reality.

Within four years, we had our first child, followed two and a half years later by our second. The highs and lows—especially the lows—of parenting young children can only be appreciated by those who have lived through them with very little help. That our sex life and our intimacy suffered was not unexpected or unusual. However, as the kids got older and things got easier, it never recovered. We were essentially friends and parents and partners who lived together, slept in the same bed, and raised our children together.

And for a while that was enough.

In November of 2012 we "hired" a farm hand to live on our property and exchange farm work for rent. While I don't remember the exact date we hired him, it was definitely around the time of the November full moon eclipse at 6-degree Gemini, which solidly hit my 8-degree Gemini Sun sign and my 7-degree Gemini-Mercury.

The farm hand ate dinners with us, became part of the family, and became Jason's new best friend. Pretty soon I would find that Jason would share important news and information with Shon, and then swear up and down he'd told me.

By March, when Venus squared Pluto, I had started to realize that the reason our marriage worked was dependent on my status as Jason's "best friend." Once I'd been demoted from that position, it was no longer as tolerable to be living platonically with someone while we raised children together.

During this time, I had been spending a lot of time working through past issues, and dealing with my shadow. And while Jason was not actively doing the same, he was working on spirituality a little bit, mostly manifestation.

In April, we both had similar dreams on the same night—dreams in which the spouse was cheating with another. The synchronicity of us both having dreams like that the same evening was too much for me to just let go, so I meditated on the meaning of the dreams.

The response I got was startling and unequivocal. The dreams were indicating that while there *was* love in our marriage, we were living a lie, pretending we were happily married when, in fact, we were just happily friends. There was so much more to loving and being loved, and we both deserved to have that in our lives.

I immediately told Jason my interpretation, and after the initial shock, he agreed that he felt the same way. Within a few hours we'd decided to separate. This occurred at the time of the Venus-Pluto Trine, and the Full Moon Eclipse on April 25th at 5 degrees Scorpio, hitting my 3-degree Taurus Natal Saturn quite solidly.

As with all things in our marriage, we approached separation from the standpoint of friendship and partnership. While making decisions about how to go about separating, we were growing our little community on our forty-acre farm, and having us both stay on the farm in order to raise the kids seemed ideal and workable. I started making plans for a tiny straw bale/cob home a short distance from the main house and Jason started interviewing his next partner.

A few days after Venus opposed Pluto in June, Jason's new girlfriend moved into our little community. Not long after that I took a much needed break from house building, spent three weeks on "vacation," and had a much needed rebound affair.

I returned to a community in shambles, a farm limping along with no work having been done, and a new resentment on the part of Jason over what I should or shouldn't be doing.

What I hadn't realized was that the Uranus-Pluto Square was busy forcing us to completely tear down relationships that were no longer working. We weren't allowed to do things half way.

I had also come to the self-realization that the only reason I was continuing to stay at the farm was for my kids sake.

What I really wished to do was be free — free to actively pursue the clairsentience that I had been developing for the past year, free to actively pursue rediscovering myself, free to go where I wished and pursue interests that I had only dreamed of when tied to a marriage and children.

In August, right around the time Venus squared Pluto again, things came to a head, I demanded equal decision making power over the property, which Jason did not like. Jason also claimed worrying about me was causing him stress. During the argument/discussion I suggested that we should just divorce and split the property. Jason revealed he had been thinking over that exact decision, and requested that either I leave the property, or he would leave. My house was almost complete, so I suggested splitting the property on an unusual boundary line so that I could continue to live near my children. He, however, was completely done.

It took about a week of grieving and disbelief to realize that not only was our marriage over, our "un-divorce" was no longer going to happen, and I had also lost my best friend in the process.

Over the next few weeks, I came up with a plan—several plans, in fact, for how we could separate without involving lawyers, and which I thought were fair and equitable for both of us. What I kept getting in response was an unwillingness to act without seeing a lawyer, and, once he'd seen a lawyer, an unwillingness to act because he didn't like the results. Things deteriorated from there, and I became another divorce statistic, convinced that it wouldn't happen to me, yet left standing with the evidence that it just had.

On November 1st, when Uranus was squaring Pluto yet again, my divorce papers were filed, and shortly after Venus conjuncted Pluto on November 15th, an agreement for temporary support, child custody, and visitation had come to enable me to leave the farm and take the first steps on the path of my new life.

While my marriage was being completely torn

apart, I discovered love.

Not that I don't love my ex-husband—I do, and always will, but I discovered a kind of love I had never experienced before: The love that happens when you fully merge with another.

In fact, I am lucky enough to have experienced it twice in 2013, but I'm getting ahead of myself.

Part of my spiritual practice for the past two years has been weekly group meditations. While some people were sporadic attendees, there were three of us who were always there—one male, and two females. I counted them amongst my best friends, despite never having met them face to face. There was also a special connection between myself and the male member of our group. I could slip into meditation and reach out a hand to him and he was always there—a likeness in our energies that felt comfortable and loving.

In May of 2013, he arranged to stop by the farm and visit on his way elsewhere, and I was excited to see my best friend in person.

Before his arrival, my husband suggested that he was coming to visit in order to begin a relationship. I dismissed his ludicrous notion because not only was my friend almost twenty years older than me, he was also happily married.

The time of the visit arrived, and it was a joy

to finally get close to the energy that I had been sensing all these years during meditation. However, as I had expected, nothing happened between us other than the meeting of online friends. We had an enjoyable few days together, and he then continued on his journey.

A few weeks later I was utterly shocked to see my friend pulling up the driveway. He had planned to return home by a different route. He stated that he had returned to help me finish my house. Since I was building it almost entirely by myself, I welcomed the extra set of hands and again was overjoyed to be sharing his energy field.

By this time, my husband had moved his new girlfriend onto the farm, and living as the only single person in a community with three couples was getting me down. I was beginning to wonder if I'd ever meet someone else. My friend sensed my loneliness and offered to hold me while I slept so that I didn't have to share a bed with my husband which was beginning to feel extremely awkward. I reluctantly agreed and while I enjoyed being held by someone who loved me, I was also hoping he wouldn't make a pass at me so I didn't have to feel bad about turning him down.

The next night I again slept on the living room floor with my friend. However, as we were lying there talking quietly about meditation and other things, it apparently disturbed my husband such that he couldn't sleep. He came downstairs and announced he was staying at his girlfriend's house so that we could have some privacy.

Apparently we had struck a jealousy nerve.

I can honestly say that even at this point in time, I still had no intention or desire to do anything more with my friend. But a stroke of his hand down my arm lit fires that hadn't been ignited in many years. After confirming that we were both okay with going further, and would have no regrets in the morning, I experienced the most amazing thing: the merging of two people through the act of love.

And then the next day, he packed up, and got ready to leave. I'm not sure if I was making him hang around or he was making himself hang around, although I'm sure the rain was an excuse for both of us. I didn't want to let go what I had just experienced.

I've forgotten most of what we talked about that day, but what I do remember is reconfirming that he was happily married, and was not going to leave his wife.

I also remember the discussion that changed both our future paths.

My husband came in and announced that his girlfriend had suggested that he tell me to go with my friend, take a few weeks of vacation, then fly back. He pulled some tarot cards, which indicated a fork in the road—one path of which could lead to great healing. I used my intuition and saw that we were both at the edge of a cliff. If we jumped, it would not be safe, and it would not be easy, but we would both make great leaps and we would both provide healing for each other.

Long story short: I went with him.

It was a wonderful three weeks, and it provided both great leaps and great healing.

For the first time, I experienced a deep knowing of someone else. I could tell when he was lying to himself. I could feel his emotions. It was wonderful, yet overwhelming. I was drowning in him, and had become addicted to the merging.

I became one of those sad statistics: the other woman who is convinced a married man will leave his wife because he loves her more.

I flew home, and went through grief at the loss of the merger. I then dealt with some shadow related to an affair in my twenties when I had closed myself off in order to move forward.

This time around, I managed to move forward without closing myself off, yet I did not end the relationship completely until September. It was then I realized that he had been back with his wife for over a month, and he really wasn't ever going to leave her, despite the problems they were having.

I also realized he truly loved her as well as me.

While I experienced unbearable grief and agony with this relationship, the gifts it gave me far outweighed the pain. I healed sexual issues that had come up during my marriage, I healed past relationship issues, I healed daddy issues, I expanded my psychic gifts to include empathy, long distance communication/energy exchange, and I truly experienced merging with another who is as open as I am.

While the relationship had ended in September, I had the opportunity to get complete closure on it when my friend visited for an evening in early October. It was then I knew that I had done the right thing in letting him go because he was never mine to begin with—I had only borrowed him for a brief moment. I also knew that I had just added another person to my list of people who I will always love dearly.

If I ended here, this would be a sad story of 2013. However, there is more!

The next day, the rest of my meditation group came to spend a few days at the farm: three women, and one man.

That very afternoon, looking at the man across the fire I felt a spark of recognition, like energy recognizing like energy. A backrub showed me that he could do amazing things with moving energy. And during our goodbye hug and kiss, there was a promise of things left undone.

I contacted him, and what began as a short affair to wrap up unfinished business blossomed into a loving relationship. We are now planning on moving into a house together in Portland.

While I wouldn't say this is a perfect relationship—he has a habit of closing himself off energetically—it is magical at times.

I have found a partner who can consciously transmit energy as easily as I can perceive it, which makes for quite excellent love making, and when he does open up, we do merge easily.

And I have no doubt that this is the relationship that I need at this time.

In a nutshell, 2013 saw me go from "happily" married with two children and a working farm, to looking for housing with my new boyfriend in Portland, with visitation on holidays and summers with my kids.

This year has been anything but easy.

I have seen myself stripped down to the bare minimum, I have plumbed depths of my shadow that I hope to never have to face again, and I have been torn apart by guilt and loss for leaving my children, while at the same time knowing that what I'm doing is both for the best for me, and therefore, for them.

Yet for all the sorrow, pain, and loss this year

has dished up, I have discovered new friends, new loves, and a new hope for what life will be bringing me in the future. I may not have completely closed the door on this path, I still have to deal with the final divorce settlements, but I'm almost there. Like a butterfly emerging from its cocoon, or a phoenix rising from the ashes, I'm grateful for the experiences I've been through, and excited about the prospects that life in the new year will bring.

Brig
Portland, Orgeon, USA

• THE WEEK •

Monday's Blessings

As TODAY IS MONDAY, many have the "It's Monday" blues.

I no longer work, but Mondays mean the grind of doctor appointments (which feel like a part time job). I'm suggesting a re-framing of these Monday thoughts to count something that you consider a blessing in your life.

If we can all overcome something simple like the Monday blues, just imagine how much easier it will be to tackle and beat the big issues!

Being such a diverse world of cultural beliefs and religious concepts, I don't know what others will discover to be a blessing. Blessings come in many different ways. They are built out of individual thoughts and environments surrounding the family unit.

My blessings are my family and friends. I know that for many, family and friends is also their first thought of a blessing. Have you ever really thought why a specific person is such an important factor in your life? How is it that this person(s) are the keys to be a blessing to your world?

To help you set your mind frame to where we need it to be, I am going to delve deeper into mine, so you can do discover your own.

Why is it such a blessing for friends and family? It's easy to say it's a blessing or something else. But the thought is still the same. *Why?* For today, I am focusing on my mom.

In order for you to understand my blessing, you must have the back drop of the situation. I am schizoaffective, with two failed suicide attempts. The last attempt was in February 2013.

The woman who tried to escape the demons of her mind did not survive—I am the woman who did, and I am very blessed to be free of the other one. I find joy and happiness in every day, and I live each day to the very best I can.

I do suffer from the physical injuries of that night, but I can live with that. Compared to what my life was like before, I don't cry one tear over the damage it caused. Why? For the first time in my life I'm content and positive about the future. That in itself is a blessing.

My mom is my Greatest blessing, not just because she is my mom. That is just an obvious reason. Deeper levels come to me from her unconditional love for me. Believe me, this is no easy task to continue to do, with all that she has gone through with me.

I was around 23 years old when the first episode of my illness showed it's life-changing head. It is a very difficult issue to the person who is afflicted, as well as for their family members. My mother has never faltered in being there for me and continues to be, no matter how hard or tiresome the road has been or is. Most people would have written me off a long time ago. I'm very grateful that she has not.

Through good times and bad times (and there were more bad than good for many years), she has still loved me, dealt with the aftermath before and after I've had an episode, and opened her heart and home to my children—what I with great sadness was unable to do.

She gave them the best life that she could, and she always kept me in their lives.

My mom never gives up on me, even if it appeared in the past that I didn't care, didn't want to fight for myself, and honestly didn't want to live—all because I could no longer see the light at the end of the tunnel.

Now I've emerged from that place of complete darkness, no longer lost inside it, not seeing a future.

And she is still there.

My entire being has changed drastically.

Are things perfect?

By no means are they perfect.

I've hurt so many people: my parents, my children, my family, and even my friends. With time, I can only hope things will heal, and that people will see I'm really and truly a different person.

With a *lot* of time, I might be forgiven for all that I've emotionally done to my children all their lives, the scars they carry in their hearts and minds; for all my mother has endured and continues to endure, while never giving up on me and the situations I've put her through; for my dad and all that he has put up with, providing a place for me to live many, many times; for my sisters that I am finally able to have a relationship with, because I've changed; and many others.

I may not get all that I hope for in my relationships, but I am fully aware of why it may not happen, and I love all of them just the same, and more.

One may take these words and think, *How is this a blessing? You have a mental illness, your children for most of their lives have been raised by their grandmother, your children have been exposed to your illness, your illness has affected your entire life from what you wanted. How can anyone count these as blessings?*

It is fairly simple. I have the unwavering love and support from my mom, and from the rest of my family. Most people like myself have no one or no where to be. My children have never been withheld from me. They were raised to understand that mommy's brain works differently, and to love me anyway.

Each day, I express my love for all of them. I honor that my life has drastically changed in such a way that people, even family members, are taken aback by the person that stands before them now.

So today, search deeply for why something is a blessing, and more importantly, *why* they are.

Look so deep within, until you see the abyss of uncharted territories in your heart, your mind, and your soul.

What you find and take from that journey will be to the authentic you. If you've never met this part of yourself before., say *hello*, and hug yourself.

For the person(s) or things that are your blessings, show them not through words, but actions.

Thank You Tuesday

TODAY IS TUESDAY, SO what can we do for Tuesday? Monday was re-framing our thoughts... There are so many "Two for Tuesdays" in the world—restaurants, radio stations, etc.—so I think Tuesday is a great day for being thankful for *two* things in your life! I don't mean the material things or the jobs, but the things deeper inside yourself.

We may have so much to be thankful for in the outer scopes of our person. It is important to us to have these mechanisms in our lives, but it serves very little for the tapestry of our inner being.

This is a little harder to do than finding a blessing like on our Monday. We have to delve deeper into areas we may or may not be comfortable with. This is discovering what you are thankful for accomplishing in your life.

I didn't always think this way or live this way. It was by discovering who I was on the inside that created happiness inside and out. It took my life spiraling out of control to find my feet back on the ground.

I have always been devout in my faith, but over the last few years, it had fallen to the side of the road of life. I had lost my way home. My spiritual being was still there, like a doormat. When I came into the person I've become, I knew a huge chunk was missing in my life. We need and desire to be closer to our Divinity as humans, but also as spiritual beings. Neither can co-habit without the other. Our souls will find a way to cry out for us to hear, no matter how closed off we've become.

As each day passed, I felt the renewed deeper and stronger connections to my spiritual beliefs. I feel they are now the strongest they have ever been in my life.

Everyone has heard or said that when you hit rock bottom, there is nowhere to go but back up. This is meant as a positive and supportive statement, but if you have ever hit the bottom, it's a long and dark tunnel to even see the top.

In my experience, it was my spiritual beliefs and being that dragged me back to where I needed to be. I am very thankful that it did. If you are finding yourself in such a state, my words to you are simple: Love and fight for yourself through your spiritual embodiment.

My life was not the only life affected by my illness. It affected my family, my children, romantic partners, and friends. They were often unable to understand and deal with their emotions and mine. This is an issue that I've struggled and fought within since early childhood—it was as if someone had turned off the switch to my emotional relationships. I have always loved my family, my children, my lovers, and my friends. The issue was in trying to understand what that emotion really felt like, and what it meant. I came across as a very cold, negative person.

Truthfully, on the inside, I was, but it wasn't that I wanted to be.

Now I find this new sense of being, and these overwhelming emotions — overwhelming because I can't show them enough, or I say it over and over, so it feels awkward and is uncharted territory for me and those around me. I'm busting at the seams with so much joy and positive energy that those around me don't know how to react to this. After all, they have seen only the negative, closed-off person I was.

It's a new state of being and I work at it everyday.

The happiness it is bringing into my life is a happiness I've never known before, and will continue to grasp onto. It has given me the ability to deepen my relationships with others emotionally and connectivity. I am very thankful for the happiness that greets me every morning when I wake up.

No one could make these changes but me. So I ask you to dive into your soul and find yourself. You will be thankful when you do.

It isn't going to happen overnight, or without you working to achieve the desired goal of what makes you YOU.

But the change will come, and when it has, you will feel and know yourself inside and out.

Flip-Flop Wednesday

TODAY IS WEDNESDAY. WHAT can be discovered on the proverbial "Hump Day" of the week? When I think of Hump Day, the first thing that comes to mind is, "Ah! The week is halfway over!" The other side is we start planning the weekend, and making mental notes of what we want to do—what we need to do and need to catch up on around the house.

So existentially, Wednesday is devoured by the focus of Hump Day agendas.

But what if we re-trained our thinking?

Instead of thinking about how you wished on Monday that it was still Sunday, and that the things that happened on Tuesday could be forgotten, Wednesday would be a great day to let go of things you no longer have control of!

It is already in the past so let it go.

On the flip side of Wednesday, the thoughts shift and focus on the week ending soon for the weekend. It's great to make plans or make a mental note of what needs to be done, but to give an entire day to thinking ahead not only distracts us from our jobs and lives, but also distracts us from the day itself. You are trying to live in the future.

Wednesday has lost all meaning due to Hump Day thinking.

Instead of attempting to live in two other planes of existence—which is impossible—let the day be one of awareness, of living in the moment, and of finding things right now on this day that are important to you. Strip away the stigma of countless years of what Hump Day is supposed to be, embrace yourself into living and being present.

Such a drastic altering of your mindset initially may be difficult, but like most things, with some effort, it becomes a part of us.

Let us take our Wednesdays back, and give it a meaning of individuality all it's own!

Let that day be the day of creating our own individual thought processes, and enjoy them!

Now that we have Wednesdays thoughts rearranging, and seeing different perspectives we may not had before, let's try to see if we can incorporate the building blocks of Monday and Tuesday.

Is there an emotional blessing you can find in this day? Something that speaks out to your soul, and in turn makes your heart stop and take notice?

For me it is the simple *"I love you, Mom"* from my youngest son this morning. You may be thinking, *So what is so special about that? Children say that all the time!* This might be true for most families. This is not so with mine.

As I shared on the last two days, I'm a survivor of a suicide attempt. This created a crater in my family life, and the trust of not having their hearts broken is still a work in progress. The betrayal of me trying to leave them is a vast, deep cut upon their hearts, and on my other family members. The simple fact that they are willing to give me the chance to show that I've changed is a blessing.

What can I find to be thankful for? That is easily said, but not necessarily easy to do.

I'm thankful that my children, my parents, my family, and friends are willing to give me the opportunity to show I love them and I am truly a different person. It takes a lot of time and energy to try and heal all those hearts—I have to approach it with kid gloves. It's a fine balance of showing that I am no longer the mother that couldn't be reached, and now a mother that is bursting with love and attention.

We are all adjusting to the drastic emotional changes occurring. Even my beautiful mother has trouble accepting this change. She's had a cold and unreachable daughter with a mental illness for forty-two years—not something that is easily overcome, but one that I hope will be, with time.

So I am thankful for the strength to keep going strong, to re-build these relationships, to face their emotions with strength, to allow them to scream, cry, and say everything they feel. My determination to keep trying is what I am thankful for.

Middle Child Thursday

MIDDLE CHILD THURSDAY? WHAT in the world can I be talking about? That applies to children, not a day of the week!

If you open your mind and look outside of the box, it makes perfect sense. Thursday comes after Hump Day Wednesday, and is right before the coveted Friday.

Is it sinking in yet how it is the middle child? The next question is how do we find a blessing or something to be thankful for on a day that is usually regarded without any thought?

Let's start with an example/metaphor we can all relate to: The world of working. You may not yet see the correlation, but you will. Let me show you the way.

No matter where your place is in the tiers of the workplace, there are things that are the same for the entire company. The president/owner of the company answers to a board of directors. The janitor has to be held accountable for how clean things are. You have the people who are higher than you, and there are those just below you.

This is where you are the middle child, so I'm

going to show how it applies to us.

If you are the firstborn child, your boss is like a parent, always on you for getting things done, asking you why someone you are over did something, and has plenty of expectations of you. If you were the firstborn in your family, you are able to relate.

Next is the up and rising person under you at work. These are the third/baby of the workplace. They are knocking the socks off the bosses, getting invites for lunches with the boss, getting noticed for each little thing. So like the third/baby child in the family these people are just like first born: They overshadow you and your work. You are the middle child. In truth, everyone is a middle child at some point in time.

In fact, we are the middle child in other areas of our lives. Perhaps in life you are the middle child, overshadowed by the successes of an older sibling, and blurred out by the antics of the baby of the family.

Sometimes there are things or life events that makes us feel like this. The important thing to take into consideration here is why you are feeling this way or allowing yourself to be put in a position to be blurred out. What is going on emotionally that you feel the need to blur yourself out? It is you causing it. We can literally be the middle child in our family, or the first— either way, it doesn't determine what state our lives are in.

Ask: *Where could we possibly be allowing in our thoughts or mindsets for middle child thinking?*

I know for me, as a schizoaffective, it is when I am in a large group — and by large, I mean more than four people. That is when I'm way out of my comfort zone, and I find a way to blur myself out of the group. I find a spot, and I stay there. If someone sits down to talk, I will try, depending on the noise and anxiety levels. I'm wanting to enjoy whatever the situation is, but I end up making myself the middle child.

Is it the person who invited me to the get-together's fault? Or is it the fault of the people around me having a good time?

Obviously the answer to both is no. It is my own emotions and mindset that caused it.

I will blur myself out in many social settings, such as the store checkout line, just to give an example.

We can find a blessing in here somewhere.

If we can come to be aware of how we are reacting to a situation that makes us feel like blurring out, we can recognize and overcome it. Whatever the setting is for you, it is possible to re-frame our minds. As soon as you feel that moment of middle child coming on, get up and move! Go to someone you know, and get into the conversation, or if that is still difficult just listen. Be apart of the group by your presence. Talk to the lady next to you waiting to check out, if she is trying to strike up small talk. You just very well might find out that things you used to blur yourself out of are fun and enjoyable.

The most possible blessing you will see is this: You just might find that others are just as middle child as you are. Maybe you'll find that you are not alone in this world. You are just as important as anyone, and the things that make you different also make you interesting to talk to.

If you really work at removing yourself out of middle child thinking in every situation, you find yourself looking at the world with a new set of eyes and feelings about yourself.

Again, this doesn't happen overnight. It will be stressful and overwhelming at times, even when you have applied it to many situations.

The key is to keep trying. You will find something to be thankful for. You may not even know it's happening. You have acquired inner strength to push your way out of blurry middle child thinking. Every time you can achieve this, you are building larger, more balanced stones to face life situations.

You are a strong and successful first child, or you may be basking in the joy of being in the center of attention. These things can be achieved with time, and there is plenty of room to grow out of the middle child shell.

So when it's Thursday, embrace it and the

opportunity to re-evaluate any middle child issues you are having. Deal with them, and don't let you blur you out.

The Coveted Friday

TODAY IS FRIDAY, AND is TGIF day. Hmmm... The reason we all say this is because the week has ended, and we are looking forward to the weekend, so it's the best day of our week.

So on Friday we are thanking God/Goddess in their many forms, based upon our religious beliefs.

I'm thinking if we thanked our God/Goddess every morning upon waking, before we head out to do our work, perhaps a Monday or Wednesday, which ever day it is we might enjoy, the bliss of the Friday energy could be everyday.

I know I no longer work, so this maybe might be easy to say. In truth, it's a conscious effort each morning that with time becomes so natural that you don't even have to think about it.

Fridays bring so many things to the table. There is the obvious Friday night activities, even if you stay in, you've got a routine. For the nine-to-five set, there is the beginning of the weekend. For others, it's the start of a hectic workload, but they still enjoy Friday.

It is typically payday, a busy day followed by night time activities. As a culture, Friday and

Saturday are the only two "fun" days of the week.

Why we think we can only find these two days to covet and eagerly anticipate, I'm not sure. Perhaps it stems back to earlier times, when life and the days of the week were viewed differently.

There is another energy aspect to Friday — The most dreaded and depressing part of Friday is for those who are alone: no plans or invites, wondering why they are home on a Friday night. It really is no different than other nights of the week, so what causes this *"It's Friday and everyone is doing something and I'm not — what is wrong with me?"*

There is nothing wrong with you at all. It is a stigma that if you don't go out and do certain activities, you must be boring. That is where TGIT comes in.

Look deep into yourself. Does it really matter that you are at home? I'm not going to recommend that you join a book club, or take a cooking class on Fridays. Why? Because you can do that any day of the week, too.

One of the greatest blessings is to be comfortable within your own company. We are so busy with the day to day that we've lost the ability to be alone and be ok with it. So many people say they wish they had time for themselves. If you have only five minutes of silence before getting in or out of bed, it is a perfect time to say thank you to God/Goddess for another day and the blessings you have within you. Being content and finding joy inside yourself is one of the greatest blessings there is. You just have to remember and re-train your thinking to accomplish this.

I know that by doing this, I am happy with each day, because of this morning routine—and it only takes a few minutes.

So I have re-framed my thinking about how I give thanks to my Goddess every morning, and I generally have days that are wonderful in some way. In discovering my true blessing of who I am, I find what I need to focus on, and try harder at doing those things.

Everyday is a day to give thanks for my effort. Being schizoaffective, this is very difficult to do myself, but I earnestly try my best. Some days it is smooth sailing with calm seas. Some days it looks like my plans for the day were shredded, and are falling around me like confetti. In reality, we all have some bad days, but for me, doing this makes it less for the most part.

So I say "TGIT"—Thank God/Goddess It's Today.

Saturday's Society

FRIDAYS ARE A HUGE deal to the week, but they don't hold a light to Saturday! It doesn't matter if you are a Monday to Friday worker, or if you work weekends, everyone enjoys the fruits of Saturdays: going out with friends, parties, date nights, having some drinks, etc.

On the flip side some people try to get so many tasks done on a Saturday that it is a domestic day of work. Either way, how you spend the day is entirely up to you.

The question is, *Are we spending the day to its fullest possibilities?*

Instead of doing the multitude of cleaning tasks all day, how about setting aside an hour or two to do something as a family? Take the kids to the park, zoo, or museum. Let them see and explore outside of a video game or TV. Giving them your completely in the moment attention that is absent at times during the weekday grind of all the things that are required of us. Build the memories that they will carry into adulthood. You are not going to attain a great family structure that would be a blessing in the washing machine. Children grow up fast. What inner skills are you passing along to your children? A spotless house is very nice, but our children need us to teach them and show by example the strength it takes to see what they possess or need to build on to have those blessings. Otherwise, as adults they, too, will not know how to find those inner blessings we've been talking about.

Flipping the coin for those who are in a

relationship, or married without children, the opportunities are endless on fun things to go out and do. Or you can even invite friends over.

But perhaps we could devote some time for growing as a person? Growing as a couple? Continually evaluate what you are bringing to the relationship, and where you could use some work on your inner being—after all, this is the person you are going to spend the rest of your life with. If you don't check in on yourself or as a couple, the cracks begin to grow, sometimes to the point of breaking the relationship apart. It requires the effort of getting out of the hum-drum routines to spread your horizons alone, or with your loved one.

Going for a walk holding hands, turning off all the distractions like the TV, cell phones, etc. so that you can sit and look into each other's eyes without any interruptions will show what you still love about each other, and how much that love continues to grow.

Talk about any growth that has altered the relationship—both the good and not-so-favorable. If you don't, you can't continue to grow as a person, and certainly not as a couple. If couples did this more often, there would be less couples divorcing from growing apart. Be real and talk from your souls.

If you are single, find the beauty in solitude, and hear the flow of feeling content within your own skin. Do the activities you love, like reading, painting, etc.

On a deeper note, find out who you are, and how you truly want to be in this life. You may be surprised at who you discover in that space.

Keep finding the time to unwind from the world's demands on you. Take a bubble bath with a glass of wine (if you drink), candles, and soft music. Make it a complete cleansing of the stresses in life. Don't let the label of being single be a bad or depressing one. Don't let yourself be labeled. When we change our mindset on society's views, we find joy and happiness. It's the opportunity of a freedom to grow confident and believe and know your own worth and capabilities.

The other side of being single is that you can *choose* to be single—another thing society chooses to label as wrong: *What are you thinking that you want to remain single?*

Some of us may enjoy a companion, but do not want the whole package (moving in, marriage, children). There is nothing wrong with that, as long as from the beginning, the other person knows. You can still love and remain single.

I have discovered for myself that choosing to remain single is the best thing for me and the other person. Unfortunately, no matter how hard I try, it does not work out very well. I don't know if it is due to my illness, which leaves me without the greatest intimacy skills, or that I require a lot of personal space. It is most likely the combination of both. The important thing is I'm thankful for being real with myself. I am very comfortable and happy with my choice.

The Beauty of Diversity Sunday

WELL, WE HAVE REACHED the end of the week — or the beginning, depending how you view it.

Typically, Sunday is a day of worship. We go to praise our God or God/Goddess. The belief systems are different and the same.

On this day, many get up, get dressed, and head out to their place of worship to show their devotions. It is usually followed by breaking bread with family and friends.

Others give thanks and blessings, light incense and show devotions privately in our homes, as unfortunately there are no places to go to. The point is we all our praising that which we believe in.

Now, let's look deeper into the meaning of what we all do on Sunday, and the rest of the week.

Some will go about their week still showing their devotion and love for their beliefs. Others will go about their week without much thought about it. Some fall somewhere in the middle. The question here is to look within, and see for yourself what and how you worship—your spiritualism. I know people who fall in all of the aforementioned ways, and that is every person's right to choose. Religion is not a job; it is the light within you.

I would like to delve into the idea that there is only one way to revel in our devotions. For me, there is no difference in how I view my spiritual beliefs and others. I respect and accept all the paths that Divinity lights as the way for all of us to see the Universal love of the Higher Being. In the many beautiful forms, it is loved across all cultures. We have Christianity, Buddhism, Islam, Paganism, Hinduism, etc—a very diverse world of love for Divinity. No one is right or wrong. Our spirit lights the way to which we ascend to, and walk our individual paths.

I think and feel it would be a more beautiful world if everyone could respect others, or at least show tolerance for all those on their journeys to enlightenment.

There are many issues in the realm of religion. The first step is looking within to see where your blessings will lead you. There is no black or white or grey areas—there is only you. You are the only one to feel your way into the Cosmos and know what is right for you.

I watched a movie this morning called

Beautiful Creatures. Of course, Hollywood made the young girl coming of age to be a caster — a witch — and tells of the mortal boy she falls in love with. Before I go any further, I'd like to set the record straight. 1.) No human is immortal, 2.) No human can cause lightning or other weather phenomenon, and 3.) There are dark souls and light souls in every religious belief system. I only mention the movie for a part that was said by the young boy to the seer that is trying to help them, and is confused by the seer's beliefs:

Boy: What I can't figure is you go to church every Sunday. How do you believe in all this and still believe in God?
Seer: God created all things didn't He? It's only man who goes and decides which ones are mistakes.

This made me think and look at things from a perspective of acceptance. I already had seen things this way, but now it is clearer and deeper within in me. I am thankful that my beliefs, my spiritualism, and my religion uplift me when it is questioned or looked down upon. I feel very strongly that my faith is not the only one. Nor do I feel adversity towards an entire faith due to one person. There are bad apples in every scope of life. If your inner being has been blessed enough to see and accept this, you are a step ahead of most people.

Even within ourselves, we have to accept and stand by our choice of faith, to stand with a happy heart filled with love for our faith.

How can this be accomplished? As I said before, with acceptance, and tolerance. If every person could think this way, we all would possess a state of being that would be a blessing and full of thankfulness.

The Beauty of Diversity Sunday has the greatest potential to bring beings of light together, or the power to rip apart nations. We see how the latter has worked so far.

Maybe one day we will have all paths walking in the same direction, with the same purpose, and have diverse levels of devotion, regardless of how they perceive the Holy Light of Faith.

Monica Roller
Oklahoma, USA

• BENEVOLENT MESSAGE •

THERE IS AN INTUITIVE feeling that you cannot ignore, and it's time to solve the dilemma of your soul.

You're more than just a body.

If you took a poll of humanity, you would get an almost 80% agreement, that you go some place after you die.

This is your intuition.

This starts the search for where you're going. Those who are more intellectual and free thinkers when it comes to spirituality, want to know more. They want to know where you came from.

The ones who have figured it out know: it's a circle.

In the process of this, humans have

discovered they have multiple consciousnesses—the corporal body, the intelligent body, and the Higher-Self, all existing in you.

What you read here is real, but there is no invention known to humanity going to prove it. Instead, there is a "discernment engine" that occurs in every single human being that can detect if this is channeling or not. This is the engine I invite you to discern now, for the man writing this has multiple consciousnesses, which means that he is aware of opening the portal to the Higher-Self and allowing the messages to come through. An agreement to ascend through the love of God, so that there would be no bias, there would be no filter—an acknowledgment of the creative source within. This is what the ancients did. They knew how to move in and out of the conscious body. This is not new. Channeling has been available and has been the way of it, since humanity began.

So don't mystify this into something that is new and odd, when it is your lineage. It's something I invite you to relearn in my story of 2013.

Last year, 2013, I found the love of God inside me.

Like many, I viewed myself as separate from the love of God. Now, for the first time in my life, I found a connection with that part of me that knows all about who I am.

This part is called the Higher-Self.

Now listen here, Reader, you may not know my history up to this point—it doesn't matter. To create a zero point, where my logic can come forward and look at everything as it is, not what you were taught it is, I didn't have to die and come back for me to see what's really there. The ability to change and almost be reborn into a higher consciousness while remaining on the planet is something human beings are known for—to have the courage to allow the reaching Higher-Self to come through the door and give me attributes I never knew were there before.

First, it's you.

Second, the system is beautiful beyond belief.

Third, it has nothing to do with victimization.

To make the story balanced, I must explain how I discovered the love of God. I am twenty-seven years old now, the eldest brother of three. I have lived in Sacramento, California, for most of my life.

At age twenty-two, I got a degree and pursued a sales career. I was living away from my parents, living the fast-paced life. I learned so much as a young entrepreneur. I can interview, manage teams of people, and inspire people to reach their goals. It's fulfilling to know that people are impacted in a positive way by listening and caring.

I approached life proudly, knowing that I can teach anybody how to make money doing face to face sales. I traveled to Puerto Rico, New York, Dallas, and Chicago while running my own business. During this time, I lost total connection with my family. While I was gone, there were so many dysfunctional things going on. I would only call once every other month because I felt like I was too busy. I felt like they thought I cared too much about my career, so I had resentment and resistance in my heart toward them.

Things at home were out of sight. Unknowingly, my parents almost got a divorce, my brother was incarcerated for a short period of time, and my father had very high cholesterol.

However, I had a lot of responsibility.

I recruited people from California all the way to Chicago, Illinois. They were relying on my payroll for their lifestyle. However, the potential of being part of a broken family affected my attitude. My vibration was lowered, my sales went down, as well as the sales of my employees. Compliance became an issue and I was left on the bad side of a powerful man. I lost my car to the police department, I lost my employees faith in me, and I was losing money. I felt like I lost my way, especially after I lost my business.

My life situation did not match the blueprint I projected for myself. There was no kind of motivational book that I could read to help me at this time. I never thought all these circumstances would have to happen, just so I can find some time alone.

I was searching for God to help me, and thought a place of nature would be a nice place to collect my thoughts.

I drove the rental car to a nearby park, just to watch and hear the birds. As I sat on the park bench, I thought about the burden I inherited, and the effect it has on my soul. My legs couldn't stand still, and I was nervous about how people felt about me.

As I gazed at the man-made lake, I saw a collection of ducks. They seemed so synchronized until two of them battled for three-seconds and then they just stopped. It caught all my attention.

It was fast—they held no grudge, and just went about their business. I noticed the other ducks showed no favorites and never reacted to the altercation. I saw balance, imbalance, and balance again.

It reminded me that nothing is permanent. I felt peace inside. I felt forgiveness, and I asked myself, "Dear God, tell me what it is I need to know?"

A jolt of tingles and intense presence overcame me as I was replied with, "If you never ask, you never know."

This was not a deep angelic voice, it was me. It was a different part of me speaking—the infinite intelligence of the Higher-Self many call the Holy Spirit. I surrendered to the knowing connection of God inside my DNA.

As I gazed over the waters, I pondered if this is true. My body and newfound intuition confirmed that it is. My body felt an aliveness, an inner peace that refreshed my enthusiasm. The depth of love I felt was grand, and made me feel like I haven't lost anything at all. I am always dearly loved by God, by family, and now I'm going home. The impact I had on my family will be further explained at the end of the story.

For the reader, I wish to share concepts, for I have learned from my Higher-Self.

Some of the concepts require you to think outside the box, or outside the 3D human perception, for the love of God cannot be measured—it is multi-dimensional, and his plan is bigger than you think.

It's about being whole.

It's about being all of you.

A piece of you exists in the 3D that we call human. That's a *piece*—not all of you. The 3D piece is perceived as complete. It wakes up, looks in the mirror, and sees it is another day older. This is the piece that is always searching for God on the painting, never seeing the big picture.

When you were born, there was no predestination that you would be here, reading this now. The old souls read this for a reason and it starts with loving yourself.

Can you get to a point where you are comfortable with you? A place where you're not in distress all the time? What is it that you distress over? Just to name a few, you're afraid of death, health issues, work issues, money issues, and relationship issues. How much time do you spend thinking about it? That's an idol, and you're worshiping it. You ponder it all the time, it's in front of you all the time.

I'm here to tell you to put that away.

Start pondering the beauty in you and the balance in you, waiting to come out. The health in you, the joy in you, the place where you can sit and say, *"It is well with my soul. I know who I am, I know who I'm going to be, and death has no sting."*

In the new energy, you can look creative source in the eye and say, *"Bring it on, I'm ready to go."* That is the light worker inside of you that must come out for the next step to be accomplished. For this is when the work begins.

Now, if you wish to ascend, give permission to change. Give permission for spirit to change what you can conceive. For human free choice can only choose what they can conceive. Mice have free choice too, as they go through trial and error in a maze. However, never once did it cross their minds to get rid of the maze. I'm asking you to think outside the box — outside the 3D cellular structure, because the system is not singular. It is all connected. Do not ask, how many? How? What are their names, or the beginnings and ends? Don't separate, categorize, and order based on importance because it is like asking to take the salt out of the soup. You can't—it's part of a whole.

When you come into this earth, part of you stays in the cave of creation that you call heaven. This part of you, called the Higher-Self, is the spiritual parent of your soul. It knows who you are and the decisions you made. The Higher-Self knows all about who you've been because it was there for all of them.

What I'm saying is, you're never alone. You are multi-dimensional. Humans have universal energy supporting them and recognizing them for their awareness. It comes in the form of intuition, inspired thought, and yes, even the tingles.

The Higher-Self is consciousness, so it disappears when humans fall unconscious. It is the truth, through the lens of love and compassion.

The human conscious is the doorway to God, and if you let the door open, the light of God will shine through forever, if you allow it. The quantum part of your DNA, your consciousness, creates emotions that carry with them vibrations that effect the way you feel. Feelings are the human intent that creates manifestations and synchronizes with others with a complimenting feeling—that's how you meet the person you never thought you would. Understand that most humans don't do it this way because humans view themselves as being disconnected from God.

Just like every human has a Higher-Self, every human also has an Akashic record, otherwise known as "human past lives." It is a record of decisions you made. The Akash is in your DNA. It imprints itself so you can use it later. Your conscious, your Higher-Self, has access to your best and worst attributes of the past. You can choose which attributes are on top, and which ones you want to inherit. You come and you go, you come and you go, until you awaken in one lifetime. Then everything you are learning spiritually will never have to be relearned again.

It's multi-dimensional, it's quantum, and that's how powerful you are.

The human, if they ask, can activate the things and talents inside, to claim the strengths of your past lives and utilize them now. Remember being a child without a worry in the world? The joy, the freedom, the laughter—claim it, and be it.

As I channel the energies of the Merkaba, I feel my way into the pineal gland, and see informational light and expansion of all that is me. It's called channeling, and it's natural.

The 3D mind was taught to do this at times of

meditation, or one day and not the others.

How 3D are you? You are a piece of God, and if you're a piece of God, you always will be. It is a circle of time without a break. God is forever, and since you are a piece of God, that would explain why we are eternal, does it not? The 3D human mind does not have the capability of conceiving something that has no beginning. The time-based reality has something to do with it. Spirit is always available for you to use, if you choose. It takes courage, just to ask.

Before I continue, ask yourself these questions: Am I alone? When I die, is that it? Who Am I? Am I born to struggle? Do I fear? Does God punish? Does God judge? Do I judge? Do I deserve love? Who is it that knows, that I am thinking? Do I believe in karma? Do I belong to God? Am I coming back? Do I separate things?

Eventually, you will find peace with all these questions. It's time to dispel that part of you that doesn't want to come back, because it's too hard.

When you overcome duality, what will occur to you is this: "I love this place, and I'll be back wiser than before." And you will. You will be back with others that love this place. Then you're going to accomplish so much more without the issues that faced you this time. That's in the DNA, and that's good news.

Not all the readers have awakened lately. You

will know when you are comfortable with your wisdom, and you don't have to figure things out anymore. You assume love, and expect synchronicity in all situations. The creation occurs when human intent works with source energy. Human nature is moving in this direction.

When you know you're part of the creator, you no longer thank God when things go well, and blame the devil when they go wrong. That does not empower the human — responsibility of creation does. In an old energy, when bad things happen, it was you, and when good things happen, it was God. You know I'm right.

I want to explain the old system humans are in. The old system has you react to Karma. Karma is incomplete energy of an expression in the past. That is to say that you come in incomplete. In a way, humans have to go through life lessons to complete things that were not complete before. That you must struggle or survive to learn never-ending lessons. Victimization is what it is.

When good things happen, it was good luck, coincidence, or God's blessings. When bad things happen, it was bad luck, karma, or the devil. Under this system, you're a victim of chance and that does not empower the human. God does not want you to struggle. You can choose to drop karma and take accountability for your creations, or justify karma with your intellect, and live in fear — to live in survival, and live in separation. It's what you've been taught; it's what you know.

One of your most common hurdles to your enlightenment is fear.

There is a lot of fear: the news, the economy — there is uncertainty, and people are afraid.

So many people are stuck in an energy of worry about their finances. It's understandable, for it affects the way we live, and the ability to take care of our children. We worry if our jobs are secure, and whether we will have our car or house or not.

These things seem material, but they generate fear. To be more clear, you live in a society where these things work for you, and they are necessary for you to have. Spirit understands that you have to go to work and provide food, cooling, and heat. The love of God understands that you must move forward for you to raise your children. It is not materialistic for you to be part of a culture and live in it. God sees this, honors the process, and knows who you are.

Dear human, you have hope, perception, expectation, intuition, and drive towards an economy with integrity. Until then, there is fear.

What is fear? You have to know this, because humans consider it to be a grand and great balancer of humanity, and assign energies to it.

I'll tell you what fear is: fear is the absence of God. Remember this.

It's like a hole you fall into because you took away God. Every single human being has free choice to remove God from their life at any moment if they wish, and also the freedom to put it back. Nothing is permanent at all. Free choice is that way.

Duality hides divinity, so it's ok to see-saw between enlightenment and darkness. There is nothing wrong with you, if that is what's going on.

Those who find the light do so with difficulty, for it is not their state of being. It *becomes* their state of being, the more you spend time in the light. Then it is you, then it affects you, and then you become it. Then you are the light, and fear has no power, it is the absence of power.

These things that are fearful can unbalance a human in a moment. They are always there as long as you are human. Blessed is the human who fills themselves with the love of God so much so, that the jar is always full.

If your spiritual jar is full, you will feel no imbalance.

Every once in a while, the jar gets unbalanced, and tips. It then flows in the darkness into the emptiness, and there is drama, fear, and imbalance, because you don't have what you used to.

What do you do? Turn up the spigot, and fill up the jar fast.

But that's what's hard.

Don't sit in fear. Next time say, "Don't worry, it will probably never happen anyway," and then remember you are dearly loved by God.

God does not want you to live in fear, so here are a couple concepts that allowed me to dissolve it for myself.

The first concept has to do with connection, and that is to say, immerse yourself with God. Visualize swimming with spirit, with universal truth. You swim so much that you will never be dry, and you will always be wet with the love of God. No matter what you do and where you go, stay immersed. God is the creator, so acknowledge God's creation all around you. Stay present, and feel the connection without labeling, counting, judging, and separating. Ask yourself, "Dear God, are you there?" Let the answer resound in you.

The second concept is to beat up your intellect. There is a time and a place for it, but don't let it take control of your spiritual life. Think high, think free, and think about the things you're supposed to think about—the meaning of who you are, and the meaning of life. Don't let the intellect talk you out of the love of God. Beat the intellect up, if you have to, for if you don't, it will take over, and it will tell you there is a reason to be afraid. It will give you a list from the subconscious mind about why it's ok to be fearful.

The third concept is to make no assumptions. When you know there is a certain amount of time till your destination or situation occurs, the human treats the moment like a means to an end, not knowing they are drawing what they feel to them. There is dissatisfaction, boredom, anxiety, and fear that things won't go the way you assumed or expected. So no matter how the situation is when it arrives, it will never be exactly the way you thought, so there is disappointment.

The *now* is your point of power.

The future and the past disengage the Higher-Self, and fall under the control of the preconditioned mind. If you make no assumptions and just be, there will be presence, there will be connection, and there will be a knowing that everything is all right. If you must assume, assume love, assume synchronization, and assume joy.

Human consciousness has come a long way. To give you better understanding, imagine a scenario where Christopher Columbus came in a ship today, and your task is to explain the internet to him. No matter how long you sat, it is impossible for him to understand the concept. For the consciousness of Columbus, in his time, in his reality, can never mesh with what you know. This must make sense for you, so you can understand the potentials that lie ahead: a softer planet, slow to anger, and more aware of what's inside, where there is no judgment, no approval or disapproval, and no fear—a benevolent essence of love and compassion that makes you realize that it's different than what you were taught. There will be nothing to kill or die for. It's not about separation or survival.

Let me be more specific so that you know what I'm talking about.

As humans, we are stuck in a paradigm of perception. Humans align things so that you are satisfied with the linearity, and compartmentalize what is perceived. Even though some concepts are not that way, they make them that way. So right now, it is absolutely normal behavior to separate things. We separate to survive.

For example, without offending anyone or hurting anyone's heart, you meet a man wearing a head cover. Let's discuss your thinking process. The head cover would indicate his belief system and where he's from. It also indicates his lineage of what he believes. So what do you do? Normally, you go another way. Perhaps he's from the Middle East. It's a little uncomfortable there. There are many in the Middle East who wear the head cover. Everything in your body, and everything that your brain was taught to do is separate him from you. The brain just starts ticking off the reasoning: you don't have anything in common, you don't believe what he believes, you are free, and he's not.

Do you understand? That's separation.

It is intuitive, it is survival. It's going to take different thinking to change that.

Let's pretend you figure it out. When you meet the man with the head cover, in his reality, it's his way of honoring the God inside him. That's it. He believes in God, and so do you. He honors God so much, he doesn't care what people think. That's a little like you — you're not afraid of what you believe in either. You've got something in common with this man.

Did you know he expects you to walk away? He's seen it over and over again, and instead, what do you do? You shake his hand, you look into his eyes, you greet the God in him and the God in you. You don't even have to talk about it or be friends. What do you think his reaction is? He sees a balanced person who doesn't care about the head covering. *"He's not even asking, and he behaved like a friend!"*

What happened? Not only did you change your paradigm, you changed his. This is the new human — one with spiritual maturity.

Is the God in you able to do that? Yes.

As I close, there will come a time, where there will be an invention that we will measure civilization from. Everything before this invention will seem like the dark ages, and everything after it will be the new planet earth.

The invention that I speak of is that which enables you to create, sustain, and measure a quantum state. You can feel it, but not see it yet. It will begin with those who figure out how to see it. If you can see a quantum state — that is to say measure it and observe it in 3D — there is going to be a revolution, for you will see things that are un-seeable now, and lead humanity to inventions you can't even conceive of. You have chosen to pass a barrier. Human consciousness cannot continue in an enlightened state with greed. Politics will change; mankind will change when this instrument identifies the eight meter quantum field around you, for as soon as you point this quantum invention at a human, you're going to see a quantum field, and it's going to shock the world. The spiritual masters of the planet will carry the grandest light and it will be apparent that those with fear, karma, and greed do not belong in places of leadership.

This invention will encourage you to change who you are, how you behave, and how you react. This will the change your humanism, will it not? That's the invitation.

The Balanced ones are going to be seen as strong, and those who are imbalanced will look like flailing children who misbehave. Humanity will look for balance in people, in business, and in politics.

Although you love your family, you will distance yourself from them because you're not attracted to drama anymore. We will all look back and say, "Those were the barbaric days," because war will not be considered as an option of resolution anymore.

I love my family. I promised myself to heal them through human intent. Through concepts introduced to me by my Higher-Self. The absence of caring for self first, is selflessness. Love and joy, all the time, is compassion. A knowing of the love of God inside me is empowerment.

After the year 2013, my family and I are at peace. My mother and father love each other more now than ever. My brothers have given themselves permission to change, and my father lost forty pounds. Human intent is the key.

In 2013, I manifested a loving relationship, a flexible occupation, and God knows my progress. Another year of mastery awaits me in 2014.

I hope you are forever changed by this story. One thing I am certain of, we don't have to agree, to love.

Sincerely,

Edward Feliciano
California, USA
Awakening_Earth

• **THE PRESENCE OF SPIRIT** •

I ATTENDED A CHRISTIAN Retreat in Fort Smith, Arkansas, at the Saint Scholastic Retreat Center, which is an old convent for nuns.

It was four days of experiencing nothing but unconditional love and acceptance from mostly strangers.

It is highly recommended to leave all the world behind when you attend. Your family is asked to write a love note. The note I got from my son was something like this: "Mom, even though you still don't know how to make scrambled eggs correctly — I still love you."

While I was there, I think I actually felt the presence of the Holy Spirit.

It happened during a ceremony that we entered a room that I later found out was the prayer warriors' room, where people had been praying twenty-four hours for all of us by name.

When I walked in the room, it was as if I hit a big puff, or a cloud. It is so hard to describe. It was as if the air was thick, and the room was densely filled with pure love.

I burst into tears and felt so grateful.

There was a pillow for us to kneel on, candles were lit, and the nuns were singing for us.

I have been to many spiritual retreats over the past thirty years. I am a spiritual junkie, but I have never felt the Holy Spirit like I did that day.

What was even more cool was to see my son's expression and hear his words when I returned home. I have always known he was sensitive, but he has always made fun of me, calling me an Avatar freak!

So when I arrived, and he saw me for the first time. He looked at me with this confusion, and looked above and around me, or kind of through me and said, "Gee, Mom you are glowing. You are actually glowing! What did you do there anyway?"

If that wasn't a testimonial, I don't know what it was.

Later that week, I also had several people

comment that I was lit up more than usual.

If there is ever a *Via de Cristo* weekend retreat in your area, I highly recommend it!

Lori Homstad
Springdale, Arkansas, USA
BudgetBlinds.com

Oklahoma City, OK

OTHER TITLES FROM *STARFIELD PRESS*
— • —

Lightworker: A Call to Authenticity

The Aquarian Empath

Cosmic Love: Keys for the Path of Light

The Galaxy Healer's Guide

The Aquarian Path to Abundance

Root (Energy Anthology, Book 1)

Sacral (Energy Anthology, Book 2)

Solar (Energy Anthology, Book 3)

Good Night, Nurse

—

COMING SOON:

The Healer: A Novel

The Aquarian Healer

www.ingramcontent.com/pod-product-compliance
Lightning Source LLC
Chambersburg PA
CBHW061325040426
42444CB00011B/2785